Minimalist Living

The Road To Achieving A Minimalist
Mindset, Implementing Habits Of
Highly Effective Minimalists, And
Decluttering Your Home With
Minimalism For Better Living

Mary Connor

Copyright 2019 © Mary Connor

Legal & Disclaimer

The following document is reproduced below with the goal of providing information that is as accurate and reliable as possible.

This declaration is deemed fair and valid by both the American Bar Association and the Committee of Publishers Association and is legally binding throughout the United States.

Furthermore, the transmission, duplication or reproduction of any of the following work including specific information will be considered an illegal act irrespective of if it is done electronically or in print. This extends to creating a secondary or tertiary copy of the work or a recorded copy and is only allowed with an express written consent from the Publisher. All additional right reserved.

The information in the following pages is broadly considered to be a truthful and accurate account of facts, and as such any inattention, use or misuse of the information in question by the reader will render any resulting actions solely under their purview. There are no scenarios in which the publisher or the original author of this work can be in any fashion deemed liable for any hardship or damages that may befall them after undertaking information described herein.

Additionally, the information in the following pages is intended only for informational purposes and should thus be thought of as universal. As befitting its nature, it is presented without assurance regarding its prolonged validity or interim quality. Trademarks that are mentioned are done without written consent and can in no way be considered an endorsement from the trademark holder.

Table Of Contents

Introduction

The purpose of this book is to get a minimalist mindset. By doing this, one will simplify their life and way of living. You might have heard about minimalism from someone you follow online, or maybe there was a news story that covered the idea. Maybe you heard of minimalism in school, or perhaps your best friend is a minimalist. There are many ways that you could have heard of this idea, and it is important to remember that there are many ways of living this lifestyle!

Mastering the fundamentals of minimalism will be the goal of this guide, as well as an attempt to fully embrace a minimalist lifestyle. There will first be an emphasis on achieving a minimalist mindset, as changing your perspective is going to be the most important part in this entire process. While it might seem scary to go through such a drastic lifestyle change, we're going to be there every step of the way and give you the tools necessary in order to find success and consistency with this life.

The concept of simplicity, minimalism, and mindfulness is to be applied with simple and effective methods and strategies. The basic idea of minimalism is stripping something down to its basic function, purpose, or meaning. There is an emphasis on intention with minimalism. There should be a need for the different things you allow into your life in order to make certain that you have enough energy to put towards the things that really matter.

 **Actionable Tip:** Throughout this book, there will be actionable tips. These ideas will give you an example of something you can actively do in order to start presenting minimalism into your life!

This process might require a lot from you. You're going to have to become self-aware, and there will be a lot of looking inward throughout the steps it takes to become a minimalist. Sometimes, this might mean confronting past trauma that is not always easy to relive. Other times, it might mean admitting something to yourself that you've been avoiding for a while. Even though some parts might seem scary or difficult to confront and accept, it is possible! There are people living all over the world minimally but are filled with joy and happiness. The goal is to find a way to live a fulfilling life, whether that is by being happy, spending time with friends and family, making something creative, or achieving other personal goals. There is no reason or "trick" that someone might try to convince you to become a minimalist. The truth is, it is just a surefire way to live a happier life, and it is also an environmentally-conscious lifestyle as well. The better we all can live, the better the future looks for our world and our children.

Before you can really get into how to become a minimalist, you have to understand where the idea came from.

What is Minimalism?

Minimalism was first known as an art movement in the mid-20th century. Art had become very stuffy and collegiate, with many successful artists just being people that had been trained at academically successful schools. Art was all about painted pictures that resembled some sort of scene. The same techniques were done time and time again to produce art that was replicated, not standing out as much as other forms of painting. Struggling artists were sick of their work not getting recognition because they didn't go to a prestigious art school. In response to this stuffy art movement, minimalists began creating new things that had more purpose and intention. There was a focus on the materials of certain objects and how they were constructed to optimize function rather than more ornate pieces that were typically associated with the wealthy. Minimalist art has maintained popularity, but now minimalism refers more to a sort of lifestyle. This lifestyle usually involves getting rid of the excess that brings no happiness. We surround ourselves with objects as a form of distraction from our true problems. Minimalism is an attempt to get rid of the things that do not hold that much value or meaning so that we can put more time, effort, and focus into the things that really matter. Minimalists have clear goals and visions in their head of what it means to be happy and what it might take to achieve their goals.

Minimalism might be the way that you make purchases. It could be the decorative style of your home and the way you organize your belongings. It could present itself in the clothes you wear or the beauty regimen you follow. Minimalism pops up here and there, but the main idea behind it is putting focus on the things that will actually make *you* happy, and not just doing what might fulfill someone else's idea of a quality life.

What Minimalism is Not

You might have some preconceptions about what minimalism might be. Before getting started with the lifestyle, you should understand what the common misconceptions are about minimalism:

- Minimalism is boring

- Minimalists are vegan

- Minimalists are lazy

- Minimalists can't own things

- Minimalists can't spend money

This book is going to show that none of the above is true. Minimalism does not have to be boring. Minimalists understand how to find meaning and will probably be the least boring/bored people there are. Minimalists can eat however they want, though vegan/vegetarianism is popular as well among those that live minimally. Minimalists aren't always lazy and instead choose to focus on simplicity in order to have a clear mind. Minimalists can certainly still own things and spend their money. They're just much more conscious about their spending habits and why they might own certain things than other people.

Chapter 1 – A Minimalist Mindset

B efore anything else can change in your life, you have to change your mindset. We can switch around our furniture or do our hair different, but when it comes to changing the way we think, some of us want to run and hide. The way our brain operates is dependent on each and every little thing that we have experienced throughout our lives. When there is a disruption to our pattern of thought, it can feel unnatural.

There are some people so set in their ways that they become martyrs for their cause. Think of people that are extremely hateful of certain groups of people, or individuals that are passionate about a specific idea or brand. Sometimes, being set in your ways is good, if your ways are healthy and productive. Most of the time, people tend to fall behind because of their inability to think outside the box or in a way that is different to what they are used to.

Becoming minimalist means there is going to be a change in the way that someone thinks. Some people might transition into a minimalist mindset with ease. It can be like a light switch for some. You might end up wondering why you did not live this lifestyle sooner. There are others that might struggle a bit more and feel as though they will never be able to give up the material things that are important to them. With the right amount of discipline and genuine interest in living a better life, minimalism can be achieved.

Looking at your brain and what makes you function the way you do requires us to look back on parts of our life that might be difficult. Maybe there was a past trauma that has resulted in our desire to purchase things to make us feel better about ourselves overall.

Someone that has grown up their entire life hating the way they look might buy fancy clothes and makeup products as often as possible in a way to try and make themselves feel more attractive. A minimalist mindset would be able to confront that issue and realize that buying things is not what is going to change the way a person feels about themselves. The real issue is confronting what happened throughout that person's life to make them hate the way they look.

Looking inside yourself can help resolve what you might have been feeling that projects the direction of our life on the outside. This is not easy to confront. To face your fears means you have to face your flaws and the things that make you feel inadequate.

Why Minimalism?

There are many different lifestyles one could choose to live. Why, out of all the different ways people live, would someone choose minimalism then? Minimalism takes the core ideas of many different lifestyles and combines it into one. The basic idea is to strip everything to its core, look at the purpose, and find a way to apply relevancy. Minimalism seeks not to find purpose, but to create it.

It is a generalized lifestyle that can apply to any race, culture, sex, or religion. Those who are minimalist might have different levels in which they practice being minimal. They might live in a cabin in the middle of nowhere, not sharing anything with those around them. They also might be millionaires that seek knowledge, like Steve Jobs or Mark Zuckerberg.

Everyone has a different objective in mind. Maybe it is your turn now to figure out what your personal goal is. By removing all the trivial aspects of your life that do not add as much value, there is a better chance you will be able to identify what goals and needs you need to home in on.

Steve Jobs wore the same thing every day, so he could put a focus on new ideas, not what outfit he was going to wear. It is important to remember this is not the way all minimalists have to live. The idea is to just find what your goal is and create focus around that. Perhaps your goal is to create a successful fashion line. If that is the case, you certainly would not want to live like Steve Jobs! The different aspects of how someone might be minimal are different, but it is all about focusing your life on growth rather than a meaningless distraction.

The more focused we can be on a certain goal, the easier it will be to analyze the different aspects of our personal life. If something is stressing you out, you can ask yourself if it is really worth it in the end. If it is not, there is a good chance you should cut it out as a minimalist. Different feelings of regret, obligation, and other emotions we have that take energy from creating ideas should be left behind. Instead, we should put all the energy we have towards upward expansion and creating a life with more meaning in the end.

Happiness is Discovered

Many people might think that they know what they need to become happy, but often, there is a lot of misguidance. Many societies tell their communities that happiness comes along with wealth, success, and recognition. What a lot of people do not realize is that if they ever do achieve all those things, that is not what is going to be needed to make them happy.

What makes someone else feel fulfilled might make another person feel empty on the inside. Some people love the idea of having a big family while others might be repulsed by the idea of having kids. Either way, that is fine as long as that is what you truly feel is your type of happiness.

Some people will spend their entire lives chasing an idea of happiness, only to either never get there, or to realize that was not at all what they wanted. There are many people that are incredibly wealthy who still suffer from great depression that can be debilitating.

Some people might not have two pennies to rub together, but they could be the happiest out of anyone around them. Happiness is not determined by the amount of money in your account or how many cars are parked in the driveway. All these things are just different representations of what some people are trying to achieve in their pursuit of happiness.

Minimalism aims to cut down the idea that there is something that can be purchased that will bring fulfillment. Minimalism takes the goal of happiness, knowledge, or fulfillment to the deepest level, forcing those that practice minimalism to determine what is really important to them. Cars and designer purses might still matter, but a minimalist has to answer why.

This is the biggest question that minimalists will have to answer. True happiness might never be easily defined, but most of the time, it is the journey that it takes to get there that really matters.

A minimalist has to look inside themselves to discover what they truly need to be happy. Minimalists know that the key to their problems lies within themselves. They can buy a bag or a car or a house or whatever has a price tag on it, and it might make them feel good. But that feeling does not last.

It will go away, and then they will buy another car or house or bag, or designer dog, but a minimalist knows deep down that none of these things are really going to provide true fulfillment. The only way a person can find happiness is by looking at themselves and their lives and determining what is missing.

 **Actionable Tip:** Write down a list of goals. Identify your personal goal, your professional goal, and your social goal. Identify your largest overall goal, and something you hope to achieve within your lifetime. Keep this list of goals handy to reference whenever making decisions.

Life Becomes Easier

By cutting down all the extra things that are not needed or required, one can realize that they live much freer, with less stress and clutter. We might not even realize how many things around us cause us so much stress. Bills stuck to the fridge remind us of how much money we owe.

The extra garbage building up next to our bed is a reminder of all the food that we binge eat in bed. Clutter and other physical objects around our home are symbols. Every time we look at them, well at least on a subconscious level. Give that item or object attention, taking focus away from a different aspect of our life.

Minimalism is not about becoming a martyr, monk, nun, or other forms of minimalist living in which there is an act of devotion. There is a level of sacrifice, but not for the sake of religious purposes, or as a form of punishment or torture. Minimalists choose to give up the things in their life that they identify as meaningless. Things that do not bring joy or provide purpose should be purged, and instead only things that elicit good feelings should be kept.

Minimalism aims to take the attention from all the random little stuff and turn it into something more productive. Instead of thinking of all the little things we have to do, minimalism aims to give us a mindset in which we figure out how what we do next might affect the overall goal. There are little steps that are important, but for the most part, minimalists will take each experience as it comes, applying it to their overall life goals.

A Breath of Fresh Air

By getting rid of the many extra things in your life, you might feel a breath of fresh air take over once your life has been purged of all the things you do not need. We might have certain stressors that cause us daily anxiety, but when we are in a state of panic, it can be hard to pinpoint exactly why we feel so flabbergasted.

Sometimes, it might just be because we are scatterbrained, giving too much attention to different parts of our life while we should be focusing on different factors.

Many people do not realize that they will be fine once they have gotten rid of all their belongings. We hold onto things in fear that we might need them one day. We are dependent on the stuff that is around us. As a minimalist, you will have to start depending on yourself. That new handbag is not going to make you happy.

Keeping up with the latest version of iPhone is not what you need to make sure that you like your life. There are different things that these items of joy can bring, but overall, they are not the definitive answer to a level of happiness. We keep things around because we are scared of what might happen once, they are gone, when really, we should be focusing on how they are doing us any good right now.

It is not just about giving up your stuff either. There is a lot of mental strength that needs to go into living a minimalist lifestyle. You might already be someone that does not have that many items, but you might still feel overwhelmed in your life and want to look for a way to feel less stress and more peace of mind. Having the right mindset is the most important part of becoming a minimalist.

Deriving Meaning from Less

The next short sections will go over the 10 ways minimalism changes the way you think. It always has to start in the mind. You might not fully grasp everything about your life, but you have to start practicing alternative methods of thinking. Remind yourself that the first thought that crosses your mind is not always true. Most of the time, the first thing we think is what we were taught. It is a response that was learned from someone or something else, and now we use that as an identifier. For example, you might see someone walk into the store you are in, covered in tattoos with piercings and crazy colored hair.

Your first thought might be a judgmental one even though deep down, you admire their creativity and bravery to stand out so much in a world of conformity. What matters is not the first thought that you have, but how you react to that initial feeling. Practice this when starting to live a minimal life. Question why you believe what you do and where you might have learned that behavior. You will be able to discover meaning quicker without having to look at other aspects that might require more thought and attention.

As a minimalist, you will be responsible for creating your own meaning and value. Some people rely on the dreams of others or look into the things a person owns, thinking if they purchase the same object, they will find happiness. Minimalism aims to achieve an idea that happiness only comes from within oneself. There is no one that is going to make you happy.

You can rely on other people for help in terms of chores around the house, maybe financial support, or just to have an open ear to listen to your rants. You can't depend on someone to make you happy. You can't live your life hoping that your significant other will change and that will fix your relationship problems. You can't wait around and hope that your parents or peers are going to come up with a solution to fix the problem. The only one that holds the key it takes to unlock your happiness is yourself.

Minimalists do not need much to find meaning in value. You will start to see the importance of each and every little thing, while simultaneously understanding that most of the items that we continually purchase are meaningless. A minimalist is able to strip material items down and look at them for what they are worth.

At the same time, they also have the tools it takes to identify the value and meaning behind something. A minimalist can see the beauty in small things in life, such as a child's smile, the soft purr of a cat, or the sound of rain hitting the windowpane. While finding so much beauty in these small things, they will also be able to analyze the root of what actually makes an item meaningless.

Finding Meaning in Everything

A minimalist will be able to see every experience and find meaning within that. No matter what a circumstance might be, a minimalist can find the intention of that moment. Minimalism is not about embracing that everything happens for a reason. Instead, it is about finding a reason why

MINIMALIST LIVING

what happened is valuable. For instance, imagine going on a road trip with your friend to a concert you both love. When you get to the concert, you find out that it is canceled, and the road trip was all for nothing. Someone more materialistic would think about the money that they wasted, while a minimalist would look at the journey they took with their friend.

They'd enjoy the moment they have in the car with their friend, singing loudly to the radio and gossiping about other fun topics. Though money was wasted on the tickets, value was still gained from the overall trip. This kind of thinking is how minimalists are able to enjoy even the most challenging moments.

Minimalists do not only live their life from happy moment to the next. They know how to look at and embrace the different bad moments in your life that might cause pain and stress. Sometimes,

35

we might go through the daily motions, hating every second of our life. We might enjoy going out with friends on weekends, only to become miserable once again when Monday comes around.

Some people are like zombies, wandering from one good time to the next in the hopes of finding something of value along the way. A minimalist avoids this kind of lifestyle. Instead, they'd look at those dull moments, the ones that are not as great as weekend parties, and see the value. They'd understand that those tough moments exist to make us appreciate the good times more. A minimalist also knows that there is a lesson to be learned each day, and there is not a limit on the amount of information one person can take in.

Minimalists can also find the most value within small aspects of their life. They might look at how a small vacation might play more of an important role in their life than a luxurious cruise. You could spend thousands on a purse, but the purse that your grandmother used when she was a young girl might hold so much more value even though it is falling apart. A minimalist looks at meaning, not at material. The physical object is not what is important. It is what that object might represent that can really help a minimalist find meaning and value.

Experience Versus Object

Minimalists will begin to look at their life's value by experience and not just with the things around them. Minimalists will know that their extra cash is better spent on a movie or night out with friends than it would be on a pair of expensive shoes that just sit in their closet all year long. Even if an experience is short, there is a lesson that can be learned, or some bit of knowledge that can be taken away filled with value. A minimalist knows how to look for these bits of life's precious moments.

There is more to be taken from a great weekend with friends than there is a long shopping trip. You might come home with hundreds of dollars' worth of clothes, but you might forget about them right away. A short adventure with a friend could be a moment that you remember the rest of your life. Just look back on all the good times you have had right now.

Maybe it was your wedding, or the wedding of someone else. Perhaps it was something smaller, like a time you stayed up all night with a friend, or a small adventure you went on with your mom. A lot of times, the moments that stick out to us the most are those that were not planned. Minimalists know that they cannot buy these special moments. Instead, they embrace each and every moment of their life knowing that at any second, they could experience something full of meaning.

Minimalists do not always complete reject objects, but they just put more of a weight on the value of an overall experience than any form of object or material item. A minimalist might still have a huge collection of things that they like, but they will not place more value on any of these objects than they would on an important moment with friends or family.

Using Time Wisely

Minimalists know that their time is precious. They will do whatever it takes to make sure that their time is being spent wisely. Minimalists are aware that an hour of their time is worth more than the hourly minimum wage. Minimalists are not above money, but they treat time as carefully as most treat their money. Minimalists put time spent with family before time spent working just to make a few extra dollars that they do not need.

Minimalists can look at the value of their time spent even after when it might feel like time has been wasted. Sometimes, something seemingly horrible might happen, like getting your car towed or losing your wallet. These experiences can be awful, but they could also be huge lessons that you carry with you forever. Just losing your wallet once can be enough for you to make sure that you check that you have it before going or leaving anywhere.

Minimalists do not look at time as a cycle, but rather, value that is earned. There is so much to be seen in those that are older with wise experiences. Minimalists know that knowledge without mileage is not worth much at all. You can know everything, or have everything, but if you do not actually know what it means to experience something, you never will.

The Mindset Shift

Becoming minimalist is a lifestyle that sticks because once you become aware of the different ideologies of minimalists, it can be hard to go back to the way things used to be. Minimalists feel a change as they start their new life experiences, as though they are living in a way they always should have been.

Becoming a minimalist can be very enlightening. You will start to realize how much time and money you spent on things that brought you little to no value at all. There should not be any regret or shame in this mindset shift, however. Now that you are becoming aware of what it takes to be a minimalist, you might start to feel enlightened.

Becoming minimalist means that you will change the way your brain works altogether. It is not just a temporary idea you can have. You could throw all your stuff away right now, but you will not be a true minimalist if you can't figure out why you had or needed all that stuff in the first place.

The last six ways that minimalism causes a mind shift are seen in the following sections. These are ways that you can begin to allow minimalism into your life.

The Buying Stops Now

Imagine a world where all stores close down. Maybe there is some sort of apocalyptic scenario in which you can no longer purchase the necessities for yourself. Would you be prepared? Many people do not realize that they have more than enough to keep them alive should a disaster like this ever occur. Other people might look at their life and see nothing but meaningless junk that would do them no good in an alternate world.

Becoming minimalist means coming head-on with different shopping habits. Whether you are someone that obsessively shops online, always must go through every section at the thrift store, or someone that falls for 2 for $1 deals, you must address the habits that might cause you to spend money on things you do not need.

This might mean changing your perception on money in general. If you can afford to spend however much you want, then it might be harder to cut down on meaningless possessions. Just remember that while you might be throwing away $5 on something that you are not even going to use, someone out there is begging on the street for pennies. This is not to elicit any feeling of guilt over spending habits, but rather, to be more mindful of how much you are throwing away when you decide to spend your money on something you do not need.

Actionable Tip: Next time you go grocery shopping, pull your cart aside. For every five things you have, find one to get rid of. (Be sure to put these items back in their rightful spots!) You will be surprised at how much you do not actually need when shopping.

Always Ask Why

When it comes time to throw something away, ask yourself why? Why do you need this? Why did you get this? Why is it still around? Why have you not gotten rid of it? The more you ask why, the better you will be able to evaluate if something is actually needed or not. When it comes time to throw things away, there is no shame in acting like a toddler that just learned the word "why." Never stop questioning why you need an object to affect your mood.

Before making a purchase, take a second to ask why? Are you buying this for yourself or to impress someone else? Are you spending money you have or are you making a bad financial decision? "Just because," is not a good reason to do anything either. There should always be a reason why you are making the purchases that you are.

When we feel as though we NEED something, ask why? Do you need it to survive? Do you need it to achieve your goal? Or do you just need it to fulfill some sort of desire you can't quite figure out?

Create Boundaries

Becoming minimalist means setting boundaries for ourselves and with other people. This might mean no more going out in order to avoid spending your money on drinks you can't afford or other things you should not be purchasing. You might also have to cut out shopping buddies or get rid of experiences that encourage you to not be a minimalist.

Let your family know that you are a minimalist. How much junk do we have that we got as presents, but feel too bad about keeping? When it comes time for your birthday or Christmas, ask for things you need only, and be honest with them about your lifestyle. Remind them of things you do not like to avoid getting a bunch of presents that are just going to take up closet space.

Make sure boundaries are set with yourself.

Some people might find it difficult to quit shopping cold turkey, but some rules still need to be set. Give yourself a budget, and instead of just trying to stick to that on your card, just take out some cash and go to the store. You can tell yourself you only have $20 to spend, but you might go over and spend $27.50.

By taking only $20 to the store instead of your whole debit or credit card, you limit yourself. Then, when it comes time to check out, you will have to look at everything and really ask the value. Just because you can afford something does not mean you need it. Instead of going over budget, you might only end up spending $16.75 because you evaluated your shopping cart, saving more money than you originally even planned.

Get Rid of Things Now

Instead of waiting to toss or give things away at a convenient time, just get rid of it right then. After your birthday or Christmas, do not wait until months later to get rid of the stuff you did not like. Do not let old coupons sit on your fridge if you know you are not going to use them.

If you bought a food item to try and you do not like it, do not let it sit in your cabinet until it rots. Just toss it right then. When your shampoo is out, throw it away. Do not wait until mildew starts to form on the bottom of the bottle to finally give it to the garbage can.

Once you decide you no longer want an item of clothing, give it away right then. If you put on a shirt and it does not fit, just let go of it instead of trying to make it work. When something gets ripped or torn, throw it away if there is no repairing it. If you think you can sew it, do it as soon as possible instead of waiting until you actually learn how to stitch a needle.

Be strict when you decide that something no longer holds value. If you know in the back of your mind that it is time to part with an object, just do it right then. There is no reason to keep holding out and hoping that you might find meaning or value within something.

"Just in Case"

We keep so many things around "just in case."
You might hold onto old kids' clothes just in case
someone else in your family has a little baby girl.
You hold onto old crafts or hobbies just in case
your interest gets sparked again. Telling yourself
to keep something "just in case," is not a tactic
that minimalists use. They know if they can't find
value right then, there is a good chance they will
never find true meaning from an object. Rip the
band-aid off and get rid of it. You are not holding
onto the object you are holding onto something
that makes you feel safe. As a minimalist, you do
not need safety validity from material objects.

Old toys that we used to have as a kid might
become valuable one day. Maybe that action
figure is a rarity that you could one day sell. This
might happen, but there is a higher probability
that it is not going to happen. Do not keep your
old items like half scratched-off lottery tickets. If

you think something is really valuable and has a high chance of increasing in value, then you can keep it, but do not tell yourself that kids meals toys, random stuffed animals, or old school t-shirts will have a high monetary value one day.

It is Not About Punishment

Minimalism should not be about torture. Do not give away everything at once if it might lead to an emotional breakdown. Sometimes, you have to just take it one step at a time. Go at your own pace and never push yourself too far. Becoming minimalist will require some discipline, but this does not mean torturing yourself in the process.

Minimalism is not a form of punishment for the way we have been living. It should be done in a way that makes you feel refreshed. You might look back on your life and feel regret over the purchases you have made and things you have chosen to spend your money on. Do not let yourself feel guilty over this, however. There is no value or productivity in feeling regretful. Instead, focus on what you can do moving forward to make sure that you do not fall back into old habits.

Do not be too hard on yourself if you have moments of weakness. There are going to be times when you do things or act in ways that are not minimal. This does not mean that you have failed. You should not be too hard on yourself when you do make a small financial decision that you regret. Just take that experience as a moment of learning and do your best to ensure it does not happen again.

Chapter 2 – Improving Relationships

The minimalist mindset demands that you start focusing on your important relationships. This is a very important part of living a minimalist lifestyle. Sometimes, you will not be able to achieve minimalism if you continue to associate yourself with people that do not bring value to your life.

You might find that a certain relationship is actually the root cause of your spending or purchase behavior. Maybe always fighting with your mother about your weight is what causes you to buy so much makeup in the hope of becoming more physically attractive to suit her needs.

We might hang out with the same circle of people, day after day, week after week, when really, we do not care about any of them that much. It can sound harsh, but we might associate ourselves with people we do not like just because we are afraid of being lonely.

It is probably time to walk away from some relationships in your life. A minimalist knows that relationships that are not good for them should be given attention to. Instead of focusing on making people happy that you do not completely like, people instead should be concerned with building relationships with people around them that matter the most.

The reason why we might feel obligated to keep certain people around is because we are afraid of being alone. Sometimes, people will surround themselves with people they despise just because they think it is better than having to spend time with themselves. Learning to love yourself and enjoy your own company is an important part of becoming a minimalist.

When you're being selective about your relationships, it means you can start to pay more attention to those that matter. Instead of trying to plan big dinner parties to impress the people in your neighborhood, you will instead make small meals with your loved ones and play games and share stories while you enjoy mealtime. Some of your greatest memories can be formed while sharing a plate of spaghetti with the people you love the most.

Life should not be wasted on people that would not do the same thing for us. In the process of trying to please other people, we might end up hurting those around us instead. This is the worst thing that could happen. We should never risk losing someone that actually cares about us just because we want the approval of someone we barely know.

Minimalists will no longer give their time to people that do not matter. Those that are hateful, rude, or judgmental play no role in a minimalist's lifestyle. They only deal with people they do not like when they have to, and never more. It is time to put yourself first and make sure your needs are met before anyone else 's. That can seem selfish or feel strange for some people, but it does not mean you are a bad person if you put yourself first.

Think of it like the airbags on a plane. If you put the oxygen masks on others first, you will suffocate before you get the chance to put your own on. It is not about making sure everyone is taken care of and then yourself. Instead, you should worry about you first, and then take care of other people.

The minimalist mindset demands you focus on important relationships. As a minimalist, you should see now how much value there is in each and every little experience you go through.

You should also know that even though there is so much to be taken away in small moments, we also do not have enough time with those we love. Life is too short, so we should put as much focus as we can on enjoying different experiences with our loved ones.

Why We Maintain Relationships

There is an animalistic reason why we have certain relationships. Back when we were hunters and gatherers, we would often form packs. You still see this same behavior in different animals like chimpanzees and wolves. There is a leader of the pack, and everyone else underneath has an important role as well. There is an animalistic need amongst some of these creatures to prove their worth.

They will do what they have to in order to display that they are valuable with a lot to offer. That kind of behavior has translated into our modern-day life. We still feel like we need to prove our worth to the pack. The only thing is that now, we do not need to be a part of a pack for survival. The only thing you need to survive is yourself.

People need to feel needed. It is part of our core. Remember that it is natural for you to feel the desire to fit in. Know that you do not have to, however. You can be authentically yourself, and you will be just fine. We should never conform ourselves to fit someone else's standards. By doing this, we're deleting our own identities, and this is what might have caused loneliness in the first place.

Being lonely can sometimes be boring, but you should not always feel lonely when other people are not around. Do not maintain a relationship just because you are afraid of what is going to happen if they leave. Know that most people will not just abandon you, and if someone does, you are strong enough to survive.

Minimalists look at how to grow the relationships that are important. Why are you friends with someone? If it is because they are funny, smart, and you have meaningful conversations, then that is perfect. If someone continually makes you feel bad about yourself, talks down to you, or mocks you, then they are not someone you should keep around. Sometimes this might even include family members.

There is an idea that family is the most important. This is true, but not in terms of biology. There are certain blood-related relatives that you might not share a true connection with, and instead, you might have a family of different people you have met throughout your life. Just because someone is blood-related does not mean you owe them any part of yourself.

If they make you feel bad or do not add any positive value whatsoever to your life, you do not have to feel bad about not maintaining a relationship with them. You do not have to block their calls and completely blow them off, but you should not feel forced to continually spend time with them if that time is not doing you any good.

How We Interact with Others

Minimalism is not about getting rid of friends but looking at how we interact as well. While going through a minimalist transition, you might not lose any relationships at all. There is no quota you have to maintain for how many people you let into your life, or how many you do not keep up with. Instead of cutting off relationships, you might just be able to alter them with a minimal approach.

Maybe you are giving people too much of yourself, in ways like not standing up when you feel taken advantage of, or by giving them more financial or emotional support than you are capable of. As a minimalist, you can reduce how much you give without having to cut them out completely. You might find that they are not affected by this at all and are still there to support and love you.

Are these relationships just to fulfill some part of our self? Maybe you are friends with someone wealthier because it makes you feel like you are living more luxuriously as well. Perhaps you are friends with someone in need because you thrive from the codependency that comes along with taking care of another individual. A relationship should not be about needs that are detrimental to survival. Separating needs from wants is an important part of a minimalist lifestyle.

Listening is an important part of minimalists. Sometimes people seem to feel the need to "prove their point," so normal discussions can turn into arguments even though both parties are likely on the same side at the end of the day. There are some people that seem to interrupt others, always having to put their thoughts in.

This is not because they think they are fulfilling the conversation. It is usually from a place of insecurity in which they are looking for validation from others. As a minimalist, keep your conversations minimal as well. Are you telling a story, a secret, or a bit of information because you think it will do you both good? Or are you just telling them because you need someone to validate your feelings?

Validation is something very normal in human needs, but minimalists try to limit how much "ranting" they do with their friends. Instead, have productive conversations with others and find ways to derive meaning from what you choose to share with those around you.

Minimizing Relationships

Sometimes, we might have people around in our lives just to make us feel less lonely. A person that goes out to bars every night to meet the same few acquaintances might be doing so because they feel lonely at home.

They might not have any real connection with these people, and perhaps are only part of a circle of people that all feel lost and lonely. Having a sense of community can certainly help someone feel fulfilled, but it is more important that they keep relationships that add value rather than ones that just offer the security of consistency.

We might have a fear of letting go of a relationship, no matter how old or new it might be. All the bad things that could happen should we let go of that person travel through our brains, and we wonder what life could be like without that certain person.

A sense of dependency can sometimes seem romanticized in different love stories, but it is important to be secure with yourself so that you know you do not need another person to depend on. A minimalist will aim to make sure that no one in their life is only there because they need something from them.

We also look back on our past relationships, regretful of decisions we might have made. You might ruminate in your thoughts about the guy that you almost married, or the one that got away. Sometimes, we might wonder what it would be like to get back together with one of our exes, or we might feel jealous when we see that they've moved on.

As a minimalist, you can now leave that regret

behind and instead focus on what that relationship taught you. Maybe you spent two years with a guy that turned out to be an abusive cheater. You might wish you could go back in time before you ever met him. Wishing you can change the past is just a cluttered emotion. Leave that feeling behind and instead look for the value that he taught you. There is always an upside to even the darkest of moments, no matter how challenging it might be to admit.

 **Actionable Tip:** Write down a list of all the people you know, and then seriously consider closely who's actually your friend and who is not. Just because someone has been around for a long period of time doesn't mean that you have to keep them in your life. Know that not all friendships will last forever, and that's OK. You might even find that you've been keeping „friends around that you don't even like, or maybe you never even liked them in the first place.

Being Realistic

It can be hard to face the truth, but some relationships we just keep around because we feel obligated to do so. Maybe we look back on our life and see our 10-year-long friendships, feeling like we have invested too much time to end it then. Though it can be hard to let go, just because you have had a long relationship does not mean you need to keep it around. Instead, you can just pay attention to what in that relationship you were able to take away.

Be realistic and ask yourself why you are friends with someone. "I do not know," is never a good reason. There is always a reason that you keep them around. Be honest with yourself and willing to admit when it might be time to let go.

Sometimes, we just do not have the emotional availability to help someone, and that can be a devastating feeling to confront. We need to do so, however, in order to ensure that we are taking care of ourselves and giving ourselves the attention needed.

Relationships should be full of growth, laughter, and happiness. Some relationships might go through bad phases, but others are just not meant to be. Minimalists have to be realistic with themselves and the people they are in relationships with.

Learning to Say No

Saying no can be very difficult for many people. Saying no might elicit a feeling of fear. Maybe you start to wonder if someone is still going to like you if you turn them down. You might be the type of person that always says "yes" to other people, no matter what they might be requesting of you.

Start saying no. It is okay to be honest with how you feel. It can be hard to turn people down, but it is an important step toward minimization. If someone is asking you to do something that makes you feel uncomfortable, you have every right to make them aware that you did not like the way they treated you. No matter how uncomfortable it might feel, you deserve to be treated the right way, and there is not another person that should have the right to take that away from you.

If you notice people in your life are walking away as you start saying "no" more often, you should let them go. It is clear they were only there from the start because you said yes so often. You will be relieved once you are able to recognize that someone was just there to take advantage of you.

Finding Value in Relationships

Minimalists know how to find value within every aspect of their life which means they also know how to find the importance in relationships. When you can start to identify different relationship goals, you will be able to improve areas that need help and stop negative behavior within a relationship.

Sometimes resentment can blind us from finding true meaning, so it is important to confront any old feelings of hatred, regret, or anger that is unresolved. This is the only way to move forward. As a minimalist, clean out your emotional closet just like you would the one that holds your clothing.

Sometimes, relationships might be difficult, especially when it comes to certain family members. Maybe they treat you poorly or take advantage of you. As we previously discussed, you do not always have to give in to family member's requests just because you are blood-related.

However, there is still value to be found in these negative relationships. Maybe you have fatherly issues and have to go through hard periods together as you both work through your issues. There are plenty of relationships that come out stronger in the end after conflict, so becoming minimalist does not mean always throwing away things that are broken. It is just about figuring out if fixing it is going to be possible.

Minimalists let go of the pain they might have carried. Instead of holding onto resentment, minimalists will let go of their feelings and put an emphasis on what they can do to grow inside and outside of that relationship. It can be hard to let go of anger, especially with our parents or siblings. Forgiving them for what has happened in the past is the only way to truly enjoy your moments together as you move forward.

Learning to Listen

Minimalists know how to properly listen to someone and have a conversation. Everyone needs to rant to someone every now and then, but minimalists still make sure what they are contributing is mostly relevant and productive. Sometimes, we tend to plan what we are going to say next instead of actually listening to what a person is saying. Next time you find yourself planning the perfect response, instead, practice mindfulness as you listen to what they have to say.

Study their body language and their vocal frequencies in which they are telling you certain things. Watch how they use their hands or hold their arms. This is a way to make sure you are actually listening and not just plotting how you are going to relate this story back to yourself.

Minimalists have conversations to learn and grow, not to try to prove someone wrong or validate their own feelings while disregarding others. Conversations should not be about "winning." Save that for the ping pong table. Going back and forth is not always productive, and it is crucial to evaluate whether you are arguing or just airing grievances at each other. At the end of the day, you will not earn anything from being right. Do not make someone else feel bad because you finally proved your point. Instead, listen to what they have to say and make sure that they know you are there to support and help them.

Minimalists know how to have conversations with themselves as well. Minimalists can reason within their own mind and figure out what it is that is causing them the problems or emotions they are experiencing. If you are in a particularly bad mood, sometimes, you might just tell people that it is one of those days.

A minimalist can look at what happened and determine at which point their mood might have gone sour. They will be able to identify the root cause of their problem and work through it, so they do not have to worry about letting their day get ruined over something small.

Having a Relationship with Yourself

On your minimalist journey, it is important to find the value in a relationship with yourself. You have to spend every waking second with yourself, and you have to share a bed with you as well! You can never get rid of yourself, so it is important to make sure you actually enjoy spending time with the person you are eternally bound to.

In our materialistic and consumerist society, we have often been made to feel inadequate and bad about ourselves because of the things we do not have. You have to start looking past this and see yourself for the valuable person you are. You have unique ideas, thoughts, and opinions that are all valid and all matter.

You should be your own best friend. If you have to, take yourself on a date. Spend time alone and figure out more about yourself. Sometimes, we barely know what we actually like and instead just make guesses and assumptions based on the opinions of others. Your minimalist journey will also be one where you travel through yourself, discovering things you never realized.

Minimize the hate that you give to yourself. It has no value. Do not say anything to yourself that you would not say to a best friend. When you make a hateful comment to yourself, use that minimalist approach and ask why. Why do I hate my body so much? Why do I think my nose is so ugly?

Why do I think everything I say is embarrassing? Most of the time, you will realize that no one told you these things but yourself. Most of the time, you are the only one responsible for creating all the hate you continually give yourself. There are certain ideas we learn throughout our life that train us to talk down to ourselves. Un-train your brain and focus instead on how you can build yourself up and remind yourself of all the value you hold.

Having More Experiences

Minimalists will focus on having experiences with family members and friends and will plan activities that bring family together. While giving gifts is important, it is also crucial to make sure you are spending time with family members. Most will not care if you can't buy them a birthday present, but they might feel hurt if you can't show up for their birthday dinner.

Put an emphasis on spending time with that family member instead of just the monetary things that the two of you share.

Minimalists put an emphasis on spending time with friends and family, doing what they can to remain present in the moment to achieve the highest level of value from that experience.

Instead of worrying about the future or questioning what the other people might think of them, a minimalist aims to enjoy talking to other people, having real conversations that will be remembered and cherished.

Minimalists also see the importance of having experiences with themselves. It is okay to go to the movies alone or visit a museum by yourself. Sometimes, people feel uncomfortable spending time alone, but it can be one of the greatest ways to actually experience something. If you can't enjoy spending time with yourself, how can you expect anyone else to do the same?

Building Successful Bonds

Minimalists know the importance of building successful bonds amongst themselves and those that are close with them. Bonds are understandings and unspoken agreements between two people that there is a shared sense of knowledge or emotion.

Maybe you bond over similar interests, or similar experiences. Finding people that you can relate to can help you learn more about yourself while also providing a supportive community.

Instead of having multiple different friends that are just acquaintances, a minimalist will instead try to engage more closely with those that they appreciate and value the most. It is more important to have a quality friendship than to live a life with a high quantity of people that come and go.

Getting to know one person in an intimate setting might be more rewarding than just learning the name of everyone at the party.

Minimalists know that having one best friend they can trust and depend on is much more important than having 20 rotating friends that come and go. Building those meaningful bonds is much more important than fluffing friendship numbers.

Focus on What Matters

Minimalists will set their differences aside for those around them and do their best to find the value in those individual relationships. Instead of harboring hatred for a person that might be different than them, a minimalist will look for value to be found in the relationship.

Sometimes, you learn more from people that are

different than you than you would from people with shared interests.

Minimalists still have a good sense of sticking to their values, but they also know that it is more important to build a strong connection with someone than to build a large barrier between the two. Instead of building walls, you might end up building bridges to lasting connections that continually add value.

Live in the Moment

There is nothing more important to a minimalist than living in the moment. When the worry of the future is taken away along with the regret of the past, all that is left is the present. At the bare minimum, a moment is just that, a moment. Minimalists know the importance of these moments with other people as well as with themselves.

Chapter 3 – Habits of Highly Effective Minimalists

Minimalism might seem like a trend now, but there have been plenty of people applying these real-life actionable steps for decades already. It is not a completely new idea to live below your means, this is the way that many people might end up finding happiness.

Some minimalists are extreme and might only own a few items altogether. Other minimalists just take small parts of the idea and apply them to relevant aspects of their life.

How much a person decides to add minimalism to their life is completely up to them. There are many tips and tricks that anyone can use, no matter what degree of minimalism they might decide to introduce into their life.

This chapter will go over the habits you need in order to be an effective minimalist. There is no exact level of success and what works for some is going to be different than what works for others.

You do not have to live by every rule in a strict way, but even if something seems strange or scary, you should still try it. You never know what small behavioral change might end up changing your life for the better in ways you never even fantasized about.

More Benefits of Minimalism

By this point, we have listed what the many of the benefits of minimalism are. Now, it is time for you to list the ideas of minimalism you like. Is it the aspect of saving money? Many people can find monetary freedom when they start to cut out unnecessary costs and all the things that they do not need.

Some people have collections that really bring them joy, and that is perfectly fine! Just because you have a lot of a certain item does not mean that you can't become a minimalist. Just be sure that you are only keeping things because they bring you joy and value and not because you are trying to fulfill some part of you that you do not understand.

The benefit will be the elimination of things that really do not add any value at all. You might try minimalism because you want to reduce the stress in your life and focus more on what it is that makes you happy to be alive.

Getting Started Minimally

You do not have to become a minimalist overnight. If the idea is scary, you can start small. Start by implementing better purchase habits. Instead of walking through the store and grabbing whatever looks good, ask yourself if you need the item or if you want the item. If you want it, is there an alternate way of fulfilling that desire?

Starting minimally with your purchases will help

you gradually bring minimalism into your life. Decluttering a space is also a great way to start living more minimal. Pick one spot in your house that really needs cleaning. Do not tell yourself you have to tackle everything at once.

Just pick out one thing, no matter how small. It might be a dresser drawer, or a cabinet in the kitchen. Maybe it is just an old box in the basement you need to look through. Go through the area gradually if you have to, setting easy and achievable goals so you start off on the right path. If you try too hard to give yourself huge goals in a short amount of time, you are setting yourself up for failure.

A big purge might be in order after you have gradually started living more minimally. Maybe this includes clearing out entire rooms, storage areas, or attics. Look at the biggest area of clutter in your home to determine what project really needs your attention. Some people might just have to clear out entire spaces in their house. Going minimalist with someone else is a great way to make sure both of you stay motivated! The two of you, whether it is a sibling, spouse, friend, or other family member, can work together to clear out spaces that need to be decluttered.

You can put on music and find ways to make the decluttering process more fun together. Having someone else's space to declutter might help you find ways of organizing you would not think of in the first place. It is also easy to distract ourselves with what other people need to do, so helping them out is a way to ensure that you can get some help back as well! Making promises with someone else is a great way to stay motivated and telling someone else your goals can make you more accountable if you are slacking behind.

Some people find effectiveness in going cold-turkey. If you are not scared of a challenge, try giving everything away. If you are in the market for a new living space, you could also take this opportunity to buy something small that you do not need. By doing this, you have the ability to force yourself to have to get rid of things to make sure that the clutter does not follow you to your new home.

If you find yourself unhappy, you could always look into investing in a tiny home. This would give you the chance to have a smaller living space while also trying to place emphasis on growing your knowledge and experience. Tiny homes allow people to travel and see the world from the comfort of their own home.

Minimalist Lifestyles

Some people might incorporate just a few different aspects of minimalism into their life. Not going full turkey and purging yourself of all your junk does not mean that you can't still be a minimalist. You might still decide to invest in keeping up material objects as well. Maybe this includes a collection of some sort. There are people that really love their book collection.

They might have invested a ton of money in that collection, and they consistently keep up with it. Those books might bring them knowledge, and they get to share their favorite readings with their other friends. It is clear that these books bring them a ton of joy, so the collection should be kept! On the other hand, there might be someone that keeps buying books that they never read in the hopes that they might someday. Maybe they keep books that they did not even enjoy reading and they know they are never going to read again.

Some people might even keep books around as decorations. If these books are not actually bringing any joy, then they should probably be given away. There is no point to having a shelf full of books that have never been opened. Someone out there might actually want to read these! In order to prevent this from continuing, make sure to not buy any book, movie, or other form of media before the last one has been finished.

It is important to understand minimalism should not just be a trend. You have to really believe these ideas in your core. If you are just incorporating minimalism as a decorative trend, way to dress, eat, and shop, you might not actually be practicing minimalism. The purpose of minimalism is to think in a way that is productive and filled with value.

This is never going to happen if the deep ideas of minimalism are not accepted as a way of life. Asking yourself why you do the things you do, what the real issue might be, and whether or not you actually need something in your life is the best way to make sure that you are practicing minimalism.

Sometimes, the lifestyle comes first. Other times, the mindset is the seed and the lifestyle just follows. Do what works best for you. You are not just going to completely change the way you think overnight. There might be moments of enlightenment or some things that seem to be understood and expected faster than the snap of a finger.

There are going to be other things that take longer to get used to. Someone that makes a habit of checking the clearance section at every store might have to break that muscle memory when they are walking past those sections. Eating out might be another habit some might find difficult to break. Maybe they do not really know how to cook, so ordering out is the way they eat. However, that might result in a buildup of trash from plastic cups and containers, and money being spent that should be saved instead.

You can kickstart your minimalist mindset by incorporating the lifestyle first. Then the way of thinking will follow as you realize all the benefits of keeping focus on only the important aspects of life.

Other times, your mindset might come first, but being actionable with these different practices becomes the challenging part. Everyone works differently so it is important to stick to habits that you are comfortable with and that you know you will find success versus disappointment.

 **Actionable Tip:** Next time you are cleaning up your home, consider adding a box for things that need to be given away. If you find clothing items you do not want, or things you might just shove on a shelf or in a dresser somewhere, instead, put it right in the giveaway box. Take this with you and drop off at your local thrift store next time you leave the house.

Dressing Minimalist

Cutting down clothes is a great way for people to start bringing minimalist aspects into their life. There are some things sitting in your closet right now that probably have not been worn in years. Maybe you keep it around because it has a sort of nostalgic factor to it. Perhaps it is a great coat that is a bit too snug, but you are hoping if you just cut down on the soda and sweets a bit, you can slip back into the coat.... one day.

These items need to go. As soon as you realize you have not been wearing something, figure out if it can be worn right then. Would you wear that outfit that day? If it is something more formal, do you expect that you will wear it to the next formal event you attend?

If you have not worn it in the past six months and do not plan to within the next few months, it should be given away. If it is something nostalgic, like a Christmas sweater knitted by your late grandmother that does not fit anymore, keeping it is not so bad if it still brings you joy. However, if you have ten sweaters from your grandmother and none of them fit, that is when you have to be minimal and decide to only keep one.

Give the others to close family members that

might want to remember her as well, or find other uses for them, like upcycling into other materials. You could use old clothes to make quilts, bags, and many other DIY projects that would put use to the things taking up so much closet space.

A challenge for minimalist dressing is to cut everything down to thirty pieces. This does not mean thirty shirts, or thirty pants. It is thirty of everything altogether. Maybe this means 5 pairs each of shoes, socks, and underwear. Then maybe a couple of pairs of pants, a few shirts, a set or two of pajamas, and then some jewelry as well.

Challenge yourself to see how long you can go with just these few items. You will soon realize that you did not actually need any of the other stuff. By sticking to a small wardrobe, you could also change it out more often. You can get rid of the clothes you get sick of and replace them with something new. It is always best to make sure you are getting the most use and lifespan out of all the products you consume, but you can also experiment with new clothing pieces if you stick to a more minimal closet.

Build your closet like you might a pantry. Only keep things that seem like they are completely relevant to your minimalist lifestyle. Stick to simple clothing that is functional. Instead of having a hundred different band t-shirts, just rotate between a few. Keep items that can be worn with many different things in order to add more variety to your wardrobe. If your closet is only full of "sets" and complete outfits that need to be worn together, it is going to be harder to change things up.

Minimal Electronics

It is important to keep your electronics minimal as well. Clean out old hard drives and get rid of old files that you never use anymore on your computer. Delete all your apps and only keep the things you absolutely need. Do not forget to clear out your downloads and recycle bin, as well as your search history. Some people might never do this, and this can cause their electronics to end up running much slower.

With the ability to have a camera on our phone, we have also been given the chance to not have to be as aware of every picture we take. It used to take hours to print a picture, but now, we can take hundreds within a matter of minutes. After this happens, we just dump hundreds of pictures on our computer, label the file with a date, and walk away. What results is an overload of content on our computers that we'll never sift through.

How much space that they take up is not always going to make a huge difference, but it is still the result of a mindset that should be stopped in its tracks. After you take a few photos next time, really make sure you are only keeping good ones and not the duds. Go through them right away and keep them organized on your phone so that you do not have to worry about uploading a bunch of junk to your computer.

Limit how much content you might keep downloaded. Many people start to treat their computers like their closets. Maybe you save pictures that you think are funny, but they never do anything but just sit in their folders. Maybe you have a ton of music downloaded that you will never listen to.

Even though you can keep buying hard drives or other storage tools when you run out of space, it is the mentality of keeping too much that has to be broken. If you continue to overload all your electronics, that might translate in other areas. You might end up overloading your closet, or cabinets. It is best to be aware of this behavior, so you can stop it from bleeding into other areas of your life.

This also means minimizing screen time as well. Social media is a great way to connect us to other people and we can keep in touch with people we might not have otherwise. Social media also gives us the chance to creep on old classmates or coworkers and the aspects of their life that we might not know other than looking through their pictures.

Minimalists know how to make sure that they are only using their social media accounts for productive reasons. Becoming minimalist does not mean you have to cut out social media from your life completely. It might just mean that you have to be much more conscious of how much screen time you are giving to your social media. Try designating times for when you are going to check.

Maybe you give yourself ten-minute breaks in-between an hour of work time. By doing this, you are still giving yourself the chance to explore online instead of trying to make yourself give it up cold turkey. If you feel anxious and like you want to pull out your phone so you can check Facebook or Instagram, instead, just remind yourself that you get the chance to check within half an hour.

Be aware of what you are doing online, and always ask why you are doing what you are. Why are you looking at your cousin's husband's best friend's girlfriend's Instagram? Is it making you happy? Or are you just comparing yourself? This deep investigating we have access to can be very addictive, so be wary of why you are forcing yourself to look at certain content.

Real-Life Contemporary Minimalists

Steve Jobs and Barack Obama are amongst some of the most well-known minimalists. Both of these successful men would wear clothes that were simple, often re-wearing certain outfits as well. By doing this, they could then make sure that instead of taking time out of their day to worry about what they were going to wear, they could give all their attention to the issues that really mattered. Obama had a lot of responsibility as the president of the U.S., so he should not have spent any of his time trying to decide which tie to wear. Instead, it was important to make sure he was taking care of the issues that really mattered. Steve Jobs had an innovate mind that changed the lives of many, as well as the lives of future generations. He stuck to a very simple outfit in order to ensure that all his attention was given to how he could continually create new products.

The Minimalists are two business partners that have made a career off sharing their practices. They were both people that had high-paying jobs and were able to buy pretty much whatever they wanted. Even though they seemingly had it all, they still did not have happiness. There was not anything they could purchase that would give them a real sense of fulfillment.

They decided to give all that up and were able to transform their lives for the better. Now, they can give speeches, write books, and run a website that gives them enough money to purchase what they need. This position also allows them to travel the world, whether they gain valuable experiences. Life is so much more fulfilling for them now that they are focusing on growth and not wealth.

Lauren Singer manages to keep all the trash she uses within one mason jar. She cites part of her inspiration as watching someone eat a salad every day for lunch from a plastic container that they would throw away. The amount of garbage that some people use is alarming, and one day, there will be more trash on the planet than space to live and grow. In order to cut down on how much waste she uses, she aims to only use recyclable items and nothing that has to be just thrown away.

If something does need to be tossed, she instead keeps it in a single jar in order to make sure that she's not contributing any garbage to the world. She buys food and spices in bulk and uses her own cups when ordering beverages from takeout places. In her mason jar of trash, she includes price tags, twisty ties, the stickers that are put on produce, and plastic bits that keep tags attached to clothes. Not everyone has the means to live like Lauren, but she's definitely an inspiration when it comes to downsizing.

Mindfulness

Becoming mindful is one of the greatest ways a person can really emphasize a minimalist lifestyle. Mindfulness aims to tackle the act of ruminating in thoughts and fears over the future and of the past. Some people spend their entire day thinking of all their regrets or fantasizing about their future without paying attention to what is going on around them. Being mindful involves being aware of your surroundings, and both physical and mental emotions that come along with being in the present moment.

It can be hard to imagine what it is like to stay physically present, but it is something that needs to be achieved in order to ensure that you are living life as it should be – in the moment.

Mindfulness is something that we need to teach ourselves. As children, we might not even have the ability to be mindful. Sometimes you might have trouble remembering certain experiences. This might have been because you were dissociating or worrying too much about what was going to happen to actually enjoy what was going on.

Not being mindful means that sometimes we miss out on the important thing because we have spent way too much time in our own head. Anyone that has difficulty enjoying their time might have to start practicing mindfulness in order to tackle some of the worry that comes with not being mindful.

There are many effective ways to practice mindfulness. To start, it involves just becoming aware of your surroundings. Are you in a room? Are you outside? Are you moving? Are you still? Is it cold? Does it smell? Being aware of the present moment and what is going on now is the most important and first step of becoming mindful.

One way you can practice mindfulness is by being aware of your body. Start with the top and work your way down. What is your head doing? Is it tilted? Is it resting on something? Then move down to your shoulders. Are they relaxed or tense? How are you holding your arms? Are you sitting or standing?

Try describing yourself in your head how you might to someone that you are talking to on the phone. Maybe they ask what you are doing, so you would tell them, "I'm sitting on the couch in my pajamas wrapped up in a blanket and watching a TV show." Start reminding yourself of this when you feel like you don't have control over your thoughts.

Another way to practice mindfulness is to tap

into your senses. Identify at least one thing in the room that you can smell, hear, see, feel, and taste. You want to make sure that you are not worrying about the effects of these emotions, but rather, just making yourself aware. By doing this, you are connecting yourself to the present moment and grounding yourself in the now, rather than frantically running through your future and past thoughts and worries.

Meditation

Meditation is a great form of mindfulness and can help one to clear their head. Sometimes, we might feel incredibly stressed and anxious because we are so overwhelmed that it is hard to tell what is going on. Maybe you are constantly thinking about all the things you have to do while still ruminating on what you did the day before. Your brain should not be like a television that is constantly on. You need to turn off, and that does not include just sleeping. Sometimes, our brain is not even fully rested while we are sleeping. Those with really bad anxiety might have constant nightmares or night terrors that make it difficult for them to actually get a good night's sleep. Practicing meditation can allow you to really shut down your brain for a moment.

Some people need to remember that they do not need to hold onto every emotion that they carry. You could feel sad and anxious today because of something small that happened yesterday, without even realizing that you are still holding onto that emotion.

Meditation will allow you to shut off for a second so that you can come back more energized right after. By practicing meditation, you can make sure that you are giving your waking brain the chance to actually take a break and relax.

Meditation grounds us and reminds us that everything is going to be okay. Sometimes, our worries and anxieties can make us feel like we are just building a huge fire. Something that happens might make you anxious, and then there is another thing that makes you a little more anxious.

If you do not let go of that original anxiety, as you go throughout your day, it is only going to keep building. All the other small things that are making you stressed keep adding on until you feel like you are going to explode. Meditation helps you deplete your stress and start back at zero.

 **Actionable Tip:** Invest in either an audiobook about meditation, or use an app like Headspace to help practice meditation. Set a place aside in your home that you can dedicate to meditation only, and do not be afraid to practice meditating whenever you are feeling stressed or anxious.

Meditation might feel strange for some that start practicing, but it is a crucial step in becoming minimal. Find a place in your house that you can completely dedicate to meditation. You do not have to have an entire room dedicated to meditating either. Just choose a place that is different than where you normally hang out.

Maybe it is just the ground at the end of your bed, or the middle of your kitchen floor. No matter where you choose to meditate, you should have a dedicated spot so that your brain will kick on much faster every time you enter that space. Our brain is like a muscle that we have to train. At first, it might be hard to meditate, but if you keep going to that same spot and practice meditation, you will get more and more out of each session. Then, in moments of high stress and anxiety, you can go to that spot and your brain will kick into meditation mode, relieving stress instantly.

Self-Care

Self-care is important as well. We spend too much time focusing on others, what they think, and what their opinions about us might be. Some of us are so dependent on the thoughts of other people that we completely disregard our own. We end up forgetting about ourselves and that we need to be taken care of too, instead of distracting ourselves by making sure the needs of others are met first.

We might become so fearful of judgment that we lie about what we like or change the way we feel about certain things just to impress other people. By continually disregarding our own feelings and needs, we end up losing ourselves, and sometimes, we can be hard to find again.

Self-care will help in growing interpersonal relationships as well as cause a higher level of confidence and self-esteem. If you dedicate moments of taking care of yourself, you can make sure that you will feel better in the end, actually getting the things that you need instead of lying to yourself and putting the needs of others first. Why do other people deserve to get taken care of before you?

Self-care can be scary for some people, especially anyone that is a parent or caretaker of a dependent. You might feel selfish putting your needs first, but sometimes, it is what you have to do to regain focus and remember that your own thoughts and opinions are incredibly important. It can be very lonely to hate yourself, and by making sure you are taken care of, you will in return care more about yourself.

Everyone's self-care methods are different. Do not do anything that makes you uncomfortable and find ways to take care of yourself without too much pressure. Self-care might mean going for a walk alone or taking a long bubble bath.

It might mean just getting your nails done once a week, or it could be a daily facial treatment that makes you feel more glamourous afterwards. Find something that makes you feel good, and not just okay. Here are some self-care tips that anyone can use:

1. Get out in the sun. Vitamin D will make you feel better as it is an essential vitamin in fighting

off depression. Whatever you enjoy doing, whether it is reading, writing, drawing, or knitting, do it outside and in the sun.

2. Spend some time with animals. Instead of just hanging out with your pet, dedicate a chunk of time to petting them, holding them, and playing with them. They need time with you and you need it with them! If you do not have a pet, volunteer somewhere that dogs might need extra care, or offer to pet-sit for a friend.

3. Call someone that you miss. Everyone enjoys a reminder that someone has been thinking of them. Even if you are not someone that regularly makes calls, everyone will always appreciate hearing from you at random times that you were thinking of them. In the end, you will feel better having talked to someone that you miss as well.

4. Cook yourself a nice meal. Some people only

cook when they are doing so for others, just eating something microwaved to keep their stomachs from growling. Make sure you actually take time out of your day to prepare a nice meal for yourself!

5. Make your bed! This might seem simple, but it can be a form of self-care! By making your bed, you are doing a little favor to your future self. It is always more enjoyable to get into a bed that has been made rather than one that is a mess to crawl into.

6. Write a love letter to yourself. Pretend as though you are sending a letter to your crush and you want to remind them of all the things that they have that are great. Remind yourself of your beauty, both inside and out. Thank yourself for always continuing through the tough parts of life, even when you might have thought you couldn't. Encourage yourself to continue doing better and

forgive yourself for anything that you might have done in the past that you regret.

Minimalist Homes

Living minimally means incorporating different minimal techniques in your home. For some minimalists, this means different decorations that are around. For others, it might include their methods of organizations.

If you can surround yourself with minimalism, you can start to incorporate it more into your way of thinking as well. If you keep clutter around your house, you are likely keeping that same amount of junk in your mind as well!

Get rid of trash and things that do not add any value. You do not have to do it right away, but to achieve minimalism, you MUST get rid of everything and anything that does not add any value. This might be done slowly, or it could be done within a week. Do not let yourself hold onto anything other than exactly what you need.

Memories do not all have to be garbage, but they should be seriously evaluated to determine whether or not they should be kept. Like we mentioned previously with grandma's sweater: you can keep something if it reminds you of something that makes you feel good.

You do not need to keep ten things that do the same thing, however. Try to keep a small area dedicated for memories. Maybe it is a chest in the back of your closet or even a display shelf in your living room. Instead of having a basement or attic full of memories, condense it down to just what could fit inside a regular-sized box. If you can take a picture of a memory, such as an old toy or furniture item, then do that instead of keeping the actual object.

Get rid of old projects that are taking up space in your home. Scarves that are half-finished, old furniture that was purchased with the intention of refurbishing, or even an instrument you wanted to learn but never did are all just visual reminders of all the things you still need to do.

Even though you do not consciously think about it all the time, walking by a half-painted room or other project that might never get finished is, at least, on a subconscious level, a little alert of all the projects you have failed to complete. If you legitimately think you will finish the project within the next month, then keep it around. If it is something you have been holding onto out of guilt, just let it go.

For all the projects in your house right now, give yourself a deadline. If it is not done in a month, it has to go. This will either help you actually finish the object or at the very least, it will clear up some space.

If you forgot you had it, there is a good chance

that you do not need it. Cleaning can be fun because we find things we forgot about. Maybe it is a gift you never even took out of the bag or a shirt you used to love wearing but lost. If you think, "I forgot I had this!" then you do not need it anymore.

Purge yourself! If it is something you lost for so long and forgot about, then maybe it is a good thing you found it. For the most part, there is no sense holding onto forgotten objects. You might just end up forgetting another time that you had that item.

Reduce the amount of nonrecyclable items that you allow into your home. Be more conscious of the materials of an item rather than the convenience. Limiting plastic use can help keep your home cleaner and more organized.

Collections are fine but limit them. Collections

do not need to be kept forever either. Sometimes, you might just grow out of a collection, and that does not mean that you should still hold onto it "just because." If you no longer enjoy a collection, pass it along to someone that will, or sell the items to make some extra cash.

Functional Art

Some people enjoy collecting art, and that is completely okay. Walls filled with pictures can bring serious joy to those that like art, so even though the design is not minimal does not mean that you can't still be considered a minimalist.

There are still ways to incorporate art into your home minimally. You should aim for art that is functional as often as possible.

Plants are great methods of functional art. They clean the air in your home, meaning a higher quality of breathing gas for you and your family. You can paint or sculpt your own pots to put them in as well, giving you the chance to have some cool unique art that is specific to your taste.

By having everyday items that you see on a regular basis be forms of art while providing function, you are giving yourself the opportunity to be surrounded by more things that you like.

Invest in nicer furniture rather than looking for quick pieces. The materials of objects are important in order to make sure that they have a long lifespan and do not end up in a landfill within the next few months.

Chapter 4 – Analyzing Stuff

Everything around us has meaning. The couch we are sitting on is made of wood, or plastic, fabric, and stuffing. These are all the material objects. Then there is the meaning behind the couch. Maybe it is where you shared your first kiss with your date. Maybe you cried here when you had a fight. Perhaps you have spent hours there watching your favorite TV shows.

This couch could be home, or it could just be a piece of furniture. It depends on how you look at it. Sometimes, we see old furniture and broken things on the side of the street or sitting in front of the house, automatically associating that with something that has no value. As a minimalist, you should see all the potential meaning behind anything that seems meaningless. A minimalist will also know how to properly decide whether or not something still actually holds value.

Look deep into the things that surround you and the purpose that they serve. Do you hold onto that stack of clutter because it brings you joy, happiness, a remembrance of something good, or a shared connection with friends? If the answer is no, there is a good chance that you will have to get rid of it all.

When deciding what to throw away and what to keep, obvious garbage might not always be the first thing to go. Sometimes, it might even be something that is still wrapped up in the original plastic container!

It can be overwhelming to really think about how much stuff we have in our lives. If everything we owned was put into a pile, how big do you think it would be? There are two main steps in analyzing your stuff. Look at the purpose and look at the materials. The next two sections will go over why that is important to do. There are a few simple questions you can ask about different items in order to determine whether or not you should keep something:

1. Does this make me feel a positive emotion?

2. Is this something I use at least once a week? (unless it is a seasonal item like a sweater, sled, or snow shovel)

3. Can someone else get more use out of this item?

4. Is it dusty? Any item that just sits there and continually collects dust might not be worth keeping around.

5. Is this worth packing up and carrying if I decide to move?

Purpose

Everything should have a purpose. Minimalism is all about finding the purpose of a particular item. Asking "why" is the single most important rule to checking the purpose of any object. It is important to determine the purpose of everything that is kept, and if you can't find a purpose, it is time to let that item go.

Not having function does not indicate that a purpose is not present either. For example, picture frames just sit on the walls or on shelves and collect dust. However, they might serve as a reminder of the people in your life that are photographed, or of a specific art piece that gives you a certain feeling or emotion.

Just because something is not functional does not mean that there is no purpose. As long as the purpose involves helping you maintain a certain level of happiness or achieve a goal that you are trying to reach, it has got an important purpose.

Having a function does not always mean something should be kept either. How many waffle makers, quesadilla makers, or panini presses do you have filling up your cupboard when you make those items once a year? Experimenting in the kitchen is important. But all those appliances might be better off if they are given to someone else or are just tossed altogether.

One man's trash is another man's treasure. Letting things go can be hard because we might feel as though they are just going to end up in a landfill. By posting things online, whether it is through Facebook or Craigslist, there is a good chance you will find someone that wants your items, and they might even give you a little cash for them too!

Even if something has a purpose or gives you a reminder, that does not mean you always have to keep it. For instance, when a loved one dies, it can be hard to get rid of their belongings.

You might hold onto your father's guitar collection or your mother's Christmas décor after they have passed away. Each of these things reminds you of your parent, so that is why it is so hard to give away. It is perfectly acceptable to keep some items, but you do not need to keep everything.

There is probably a good chance that the person who passed away needed to do some decluttering themselves! Giving away these items is hard because we do not want to let go of that person.

However, keeping their things will not make us forget about them! You do not need fifty items to remind yourself of your loved one that passed.

You are not going to forget about them because you give their stuff away.

Materials

Minimalists appreciate the materials that make up an object. While a minimalist will look at the intention and purpose of an object, they will also make sure to look at the purpose of the materials that make up that object.

The more environmentally conscious a minimalist is about the products they are using, the better equipped they will be to determine whether or not something should be kept or trashed. By investing in good quality items versus a surplus of cheap junk, a minimalist will find more fulfillment from one particular item rather than if they filled their home with meaningless bits of plastic.

They are mindful of the chemicals and other forms of unnecessary or potentially harmful substances that might be present with any one thing. A minimalist thinks to the core about the purpose and intention of everything. While you can only be so conscious of your own behavior, you can still help a little bit when it comes to companies and corporations that produce the stuff that causes people's junk to pile up.

For example, everyone probably has an item in their home they received as a present from some sort of silly gift shop like Spencer's or Five Below. This plastic item was created by a company that might have ended up selling out, only to end up producing even more.

If we all stopped buying that meaningless bit of plastic, then we'll be able to cause that company to stop production, reducing the overall waste produced. Companies that produce random cheap plastic items should aim for minimalism as well, so by being more conscious of our own shopping habits, we could in turn affect how much junk is being put into the world.

When purchasing products, be mindful of the ingredients in order to ensure you are not pumping your body with chemicals you do not need. A minimalist will only consume things that are good for them, and they will make sure that they are very mindful about the things that they choose to eat. Look at the chemicals in whatever food you are purchasing and do your best to aim for whole foods, or items that contain less than five ingredients. By doing this, you are making sure you are reducing the chance of taking in something that could end up hurting you in the end.

Look into the materials that make up furniture, homes, cars, and other things that you want to last a long time. Not everyone can afford a solid wood dining room table, but we should all still do our best to avoid filling our home with plastic junk!

The Fog of Consumerism

Consumerism is the result of mass media propaganda created by big businesses to get people to spend their money. The industrial revolution aided in the ability to produce more at a quicker rate in a simpler way. Instead of having to make a table by hand, a machine can make ten in an hour.

This revolution led to an overproduction of items. People had way too many options, so many companies became panicked, wondering how to get their stuff to sell. In order to make sure that there was still a demand for certain items, these companies used marketing techniques to manipulate users into purchasing items. The idea of using a sexy woman to sell a car was born, the companies knowing that men will see the sexy woman and think that by buying the car, in a way, they are buying her.

These techniques were obvious in some cases, with commercials or ads blatantly saying, "You will be better if you purchase X." As consumers became more aware, it was harder to start manipulating emotions in order to get people to buy things.

A big example of this is when we look back at U.S. history during WWII. Because of all the supplies needed for war, and situations that made it difficult to get certain goods, there was a lack of nylon. This meant women couldn't wear nylons with their skirts, and by that point, there was already an idea of the masculinity associated with body hair.

In order to make sure that their legs looked smooth without nylons, women would shave their legs. Then, since there were not as many men around to buy razors because they had been drafted into the war, razor companies started scrambling to find a way to stay relevant. They took to marketing campaigns featuring ladies with smooth legs to convince women that they needed to keep their body hair invisible. Different advertisers would set the standard of beauty, offering the only option to meet that standard in the end.

Consumerism can basically be exemplified by thinking of a tire company that hired their employees to slash tires in the area around the shop. That way, people would have to bring their cars in. The tire company created a problem that didn't exist before, and then they gave the only solution to that problem as well.

Production is important in keeping the world running, but not all parts. Many people rely on factory jobs and the income that comes along with producing goods. We should not completely eliminate any and all forms of goods. There can still be plenty enjoyed from material objects as well. It is just important for minimalists to be highly aware of all the tricks by marketers they might be falling for to make sure that they do not end up spending money on things they do not need just to feel like they are living up to someone else's standards of beauty.

We have been tricked into buying things that we do not need, just so we can feel like we are fulfilling some part of ourselves. This is done to impress people that we probably would not care about otherwise! It is an endless cycle that minimalism aims to break.

 **Actionable Tip:** Right now, wherever you are sitting, count how many brands or logos you can see without moving. Look at the label on your drinks, your computers, your products, and all the things that are surrounding you. All of these names or logos are there to advertise a product!

Not all minimalists give up purchasing altogether. Some forms can still be fun to indulge in, but you have to be mindful of how far you are taking it. Are you buying that makeup because you genuinely enjoy experimenting with makeup techniques, or are you just doing it to cover up your blemishes in the hopes that you will look like the girl on the front of the makeup package?

These standards are set incredibly high because even the models that we want to look like do not look like themselves! They are usually caked on with makeup that only looks good in the lighting that was set up for their photo shoot. They will also end up getting airbrushed afterwards as well to remove any flaw. Then, their face and body get reshaped into forms that are not even physically possible to achieve. Once we become hyper-aware of the beauty standards that have been created, we'll be much better at analyzing our stuff and breaking through the cloudy consumerism bubble we have been trapped in.

Identifying with Objects

As we grow, we try more and more to identify ourselves. We question our levels of compassion, how much we like certain forms of media, and refine our taste pallets. All this time, we are trying to identify ourselves. It is a natural human desire to want to find your "label." Are you tough and strong-willed? Are you more sweet and innocent? Do you like pink and flowers or do you prefer all black and spikes? Whatever we like, we try to use as an indication of who we are in order to figure out our place in life.

In our capitalist society, we have been branding ourselves, or rather, identifying ourselves with various objects. Maybe it is through sports memorabilia, or a unique record collection. Our collections and the things we like to have and purchase might start creating our identity.

This is how we see ourselves as well as the way that other people see us. Our identities can be easy ways for other people to try and grasp how we might react to certain things, or where we might feel comfortable fitting in.

There is nothing wrong with identifying yourself with the things you like. It is a tool we used as kids and teens to help find purpose and meaning.

We just have to be aware now of how those identities are affecting our lifestyle. Identifying yourself with objects can sometimes make you feel empty. You might look at what items you do not have and feel as though that means there is not as much value to you. You might get lost trying to fit into this identity when it is not really what you actually need to be happy. It can be exhausting to try to keep up with appearances, and you will end up losing your actual identity in the process.

Brainwashing Tactics

A minimalist becomes very aware of all the forms of subliminal persuasion that different companies use to get you to buy certain things. As a minimalist, you will now be able to know and identify when you might be getting tricked into buying into a certain product or service you think you need to feel fulfilled. Is the ad company using sympathetic or other emotional tactics to try to get you to make a purchase?

The beauty industry sets a standard for those to follow, while selling you the "tools" you need to meet this standard. As a minimalist, you know this now and should not allow yourself to buy into that. When going to the store and shopping for an outfit, are you doing it because you need clothes to wear or because you want to impress someone else?

Not all advertising is inherently evil, but we have to be wary of how a company might be manipulating us into buying their product. Advertising is an important step for companies to get people to have awareness and interest in their product. Still, it has been taken to some pretty extreme heights and it is time for us now to protect ourselves. When commercials come on, mute your TV.

If you are listening to music and ads come on, pull out your earbuds. Whenever you see an advertisement on your social media, block the page so that they can't show you advertisements anymore. Make yourself aware of the different tactics that a company might use to get you to buy something so that you can ensure you do not fall for the tricks different marketers are using.

Here are some common brainwashing tactics advertisers use that might make you want to make a purchase:

1. An illusion of "choices" even when the final result is going to be the same.

2. Repetitive phrasing and subliminal messages to get an idea in your head without you even realizing.

3. Emotional manipulation or use of common

feelings of sorrow in order to get you to feel an obligation to a purchase or service.

Seeing Your Stuff for What It Really Is

Humans seem to be the only animals that like to put meaning to different things. A few other animals use different kinds of tools, and in some cases, they use objects to identify themselves. For instance, there are species of birds that will use colorful objects in their nests to attract other birds. Other than that, we're the only animals that will hold onto an object our entire life because of the meaning involved.

There are objects that represent symbols to us. For instance, the color red represents lust or passion. It could also mean danger or alarm. Red is just a color, but there can be different meaning attached depending on the context. Different perspectives produce different results so to determine whether or not you actually need something, you have to see your stuff for what it really is. Is it just a plastic formation, or is it a tool required to keep you happy?

A minimalist knows how to look at something at its very core, seeing objects for what they really are. is it something that makes you feel good, or is it just a distraction from a bigger issue that you need to confront?

Does this Have Value?

Creating value is important for a minimalist. The biggest part of minimalism is your mindset, and that involves how you look at an object. It is completely up to you whether or not something actually has value. For some people, a diamond ring is everything. Others might see the diamond as nothing more than a shiny rock. Only you can develop your ideas and restrictions on what creates value.

Ask yourself if what you have really adds value to your life. You might have an extensive mug collection, but do you actually feel good about having all these mugs? Or are they just there because your friends and family kept giving you different mugs from every holiday?

Does an object have meaning because you gave it meaning or because someone else did? Just because there might be an item that is valuable for one person, it might be something that has no purpose to someone else. Do not let other's definitions of values dictate how much emphasis and energy you now give an object.

You might find a lot of value in all your material stuff. That is fine! Minimalism for you might just be decluttering your mind. You can still buy items other than just the basic necessities. You just have to do so in a way that includes evaluating the actual purpose of the object and the emotion that it makes you feel.

 **Actionable Tip:** Using your goals list from one of the last actionable tips, now try to create a value checklist. This should include the minimum requirements for what makes an item have value. On the list should be things like – provides a service, brings happiness, elicits emotion. Make sure whatever you are keeping checks off the important parts of your list!

Your Stuff is Stressing You Out

Less stuff = less stress = more freedom

We might not even realize how much the stuff around us can add stress. By keeping piles of stuff around, projects that need finishing, and other meaningless junk, we're always keeping our brain on high alert. We're signaling to our minds that the work is not over yet and that it will take a while before it is. Clutter takes maintenance. You have to buy the space to put things and you have to put the time and effort into upkeep as well.

Your mind, no matter how little of it, gives attention to every object that you see. Even though your half-painted portrait is all the way in the corner of the room, your mind still clicks on when it gets a glimpse, adding something else that you should be stressed about.

The less objects you put in front of your face, the more attention you are giving your brain. In a clean, white, empty room, your brain does not have anything to focus on but itself. You will be able to give more attention to the things that are important instead of focusing on things that do not matter. Your home does not have to be perfectly empty either. Just fill the space with things that elicit positive emotions, such as interesting art, furniture you like, and pictures of the people you love.

Detaching from Your Stuff

Detaching from objects might be the hardest part about becoming a minimalist. This does not mean throwing away your grandmother's locket that she gave you right before she passed away. If something really makes you happy, you should keep it. Minimalism is about getting rid of things that do not truly make you happy. It might be very challenging for some people, but it is most certainly possible. You have what it takes to find a clear mind and live a happy life.

50 Tips to Help You Say Goodbye to Your Things

1. Start by asking why. Why do I need this? Why can't I let go of this specific object? If it is easy to answer why, then there is a good chance that it has meaning. If you know right away that you like having something around because it makes

you feel better and elicits a happy emotion, it is certainly something that should be kept! The point of minimalism is to find purpose and intent, so if your answer involves either of those things, the object is completely fine to keep around.

2. If you struggle to come up with a good reason to keep something, it likely can be given away or tossed. If your answer to "why should I keep this?" is because you are afraid of what might happen if you toss it, or because it might be good "someday," you need to separate yourself from the object and move on.

3. Remember that you will survive with your stuff gone. Sometimes it can be hard to let go because we become so afraid of what will happen without that object. Can you recall a time you really regret throwing something away? Maybe you had a large beanie baby collection you could

have cashed in on, but in reality, most of us will be perfectly fine once we give our things away. It is probably a lot harder to remember all the stuff you've thrown away versus all the stuff in your house now that you keep just because you are scared of letting go.

4. Analyze anything that seems just like a "prop." Do you have certain books you keep around because you secretly think they make you look smart? Do you have old clothes in your closet for the sake of novelty rather than function? Anything that you keep just for "appearances" should go. Your objects should have purpose and intent and they should not be kept just because you want them to prove something to someone else.

5. Remember that everything takes up space. Everything takes up time and energy. By keeping something around, you are basically giving it free

rent. Ask yourself if that object is worth the space it takes up, and whether or not it takes your time. Is it something that you have to clean often even though you never use it? If an object just sits there to collect dust, then there is a good chance you should just get rid of it.

6. "Maybe," "Someday," "One day," are all phrases that are dangerous for people. Saying these things to yourself gives you the idea that an object might have the potential to be useful at some point. If you say any of these things when justifying if you should keep something, get rid of it. These are all solutions to problems that have not been created just yet, so instead of trying to prepare for the future by keeping a bunch of meaningless stuff around, try instead to practice mindfulness to be sure that you are living in the now, putting an emphasis on the current time that you are in.

7. Keeping clothes that are too small in the hope of losing weight is just a reminder of the weight you have not lost yet. If you do go down a couple of sizes, you should reward yourself with new clothes anyway. By keeping around clothes that are too small, you are just always reminding yourself that you have not lost the weight yet. These subtle clues you find in your closet just add to daily stress and anxiety without you even realizing.

8. Remind yourself it is okay to let go. Nothing bad is going to happen from you getting rid of objects. You will not get in trouble, and you are not a bad person for wanting to keep things around. Just remember to not keep things purely out of guilt.

9. Congratulate yourself when you do say goodbye to an item. It is not easy for a lot of people to get rid of the things that make them

happy. If you have the ability to really let go of something that at one point held a lot of value for you, you should be proud and recognize your own strength.

10. Do not be too hard on yourself if you fail. If you end up going through your entire closet and only throw one thing away, that is okay. Just revisit it in a month. You will realize that all those "maybes" or "just in case," scenarios were pointless and now you should get rid of the things you did not use.

11. Stop behavior right in its tracks if things start to build up again. If you got rid of a bunch of stuff only to replace it with more, know that the root cause has not been investigated and now it is important to figure out why you still feel the need to have certain things around.

12. Go throw something away right now. Stop

reading this and find something to toss. When you come back, congratulate yourself!

13. Try doing this occasionally, when you feel like you need to be distracted. If you are feeling particularly anxious, distract yourself by finding an item to get rid of. You will start associating minimizing as a stress reliever and it will become easier and more calming to start to throw things away.

14. Pack a suitcase like you are going away for a weekend. Once you are done with an item, put it back in the suitcase and continue this practice for a week. You will realize in no time that what you think you use in a weekend, you really use in a week. This can help reduce your bags next time you pack for a trip.

15. Take this packing exercise and use it as a way you decide whether or not to keep different

clothing and other items as well. It can be hard to let things go out of the fear that we might still need them one day. By practicing living out of a small space, you will realize you really do not need that many things.

16. Try swapping clothes or other things with friends. Try using online forums for trades as well. Maybe you could trade three or four pairs of your inexpensive shoes for one pair of quality boots.

17. You will be surprised at how many people are willing to give away some stuff for the trade of yours. Make sure that you are downsizing during these trades, however, and not adding more junk to your pile.

18. If you have more than one of something, you likely do not need it. You do not need three different spatulas, or five pairs of scissors. How

many empty markers do you have laying around? Get rid of a bunch of trash and keep one item only instead.

19. If something is particularly hard to get rid of, just take a picture of it. If it is an old item that makes you think of a better time but takes up a large spot in your closet, snap a picture and keep that on your computer or in an album. You do not need the entire object to remember the memory it represents.

20. Do not fill a space just because you feel like you need to. Sometimes, we have storage areas and think that since it is designated for storage, it does not matter if we keep things there. You might find that you could actually use that space for something else, so do not be afraid to keep spots empty.

21. Use glass jars and canisters to keep food in.

Get rid of bulky boxes and half-empty bags that are filling your pantry and keeping it disorganized. Move products into different canisters that are the same size, as this will save space and make it easier to take inventory before grocery trips.

22. Have a group yard sale! Sometimes we might not have enough stuff justify having an entire yard sale. Talk with your neighbors or friends in the area and see who else could use a closet purge. Have a yard sale to get some extra cash for your stuff.

23. Sell things in bulk too, like bags of clothes for $5 instead of individually pricing things. This is a way to make more money and to encourage people to take more items.

24. Get rid of Halloween costumes, bridesmaid/high school dance dresses, and other

clothing that is really only worn one time. If it is hard to part with, take a picture. Just remember it will get more value with someone else than if it continues to just sit on your shelf.

25. If your sock does not have a match, trash it! As simple as that. There is no reason your sock drawer should be overflowing with things that you can't even wear anymore. Cut up old socks to use as dish rags or other things to clean.

26. You do not need more than 10 pairs of underwear. If you do, maybe see a doctor to figure out why you would go through so many pairs so quickly or consider upping how often you do laundry.

27. If a product is almost empty, it is okay to let it go. You do not have to keep a mostly empty bottle of makeup or shampoo just because there is a last drop in there. If you have already moved

on or have an alternate, just toss it.

28. Remember that spices and baking supplies do expire. We might keep salt, pepper, baking soda, and flour around for a long period of time because it seemingly does not expire. It does! Check the label for expiration dates, and when it comes to spices, smell them to see if they are still good. If there is no scent, there is not going to be any flavor.

29. Cards need to go. There is no reason you should have hundreds of greeting cards. Cut out signatures or little notes from friends and family, but if it is just a Hallmark card that is signed from a name you do not' even recognize, there is no reason to keep it around.

30. Miscellaneous parts that you are not sure where they came from should not be kept. In most people's homes, you will find a junk

drawer, or junk closet. In order to make sure that you can keep these spaces minimized, throw out anything that you can't easily identify. There might be a strange looking metal piece, or some plastic rings that might be important. If you do not know right away where it belongs, just trash it. Any parts that might be missing from furniture or something else can likely be replaced by the manufacturer if you are really concerned.

31. A book or movie that you do not intend to read or watch again should go. Any movie that is also on a streaming service you have does not need to be kept either. If there is no chance you are actually going to read it again, just let it go.

32. Takeout menus, catalogs, and magazines do not serve a purpose after they've been used. Most menus can be found online, and catalogs only include certain objects that can be seasonally purchased. These bits of paper should simply be

recycled.

33. More than one pair of old glasses is not necessary to keep. The same goes for sunglasses. If you rely desperately on your prescription, you should keep an extra pair to hold you over if your current ones break but reading glasses or anything else that you do not wear should be tossed.

34. Anything that is broken, ripped, torn, filled with holes, or unfixable should be thrown away. These items would fall into the category of "maybe" or "someday," so there is no reason to keep them around.

35. Electronics that are not currently being used should go as well. We might have old computers in the basement or drawers full of miscellaneous cables that we keep around "just in case." Most of the time, we'll buy cables and cords as we need

them. Old computers can be professionally recycled as well, so no one should be afraid of giving these items up.

36. Any receipts that are older than a month should be tossed, and this goes for anything that was purchased on a small level. If you purchased clothes you might return or a gift, you could keep it around, but do not stuff your drawers full of Starbucks receipts, as you will never need these.

37. Try to tell the people at the cash registers where you are purchasing items that you do not want a receipt at all in order to save on paper.

38. Old sheets and curtains might take up shelf space in our cupboards, but we rarely ever use these items again. One set of backup sheets might be helpful, especially if you have kids, but there is no reason to have a bunch of mismatched pillowcases and fitted sheets, or

curtains that do not even go with your current windows.

39. Remember to downsize on blankets as well. As we purchase new comforters, duvets, and throw blankets, the pile of old blankets can quickly grow. Unless you plan on starting a refugee camp in your living room, there is no reason anyone would need more than a couple of throw blankets.

40. Appliances that only have one purpose might be filling up our kitchen cabinets, but in reality, we rarely use them. Instead of buying a smoothie blender, food processor, or sorbet maker, try investing in one appliance that could do all of those things. If you have made waffles once in the past year, there is really no need to keep that waffle maker around.

41. Downsize on the number of scarves, hats,

gloves, and other winter gear you have. The same goes for your bathing suit. You only need one of these and maybe one as a backup. There is no need to keep your swimsuits from the past five years.

42. Picture duplicates can be trashed or recycled as well. In the age of digital cameras, there is not as much of a need for all our different printed pictures. Disposable camera times might have led to us printing way more copies of certain photographs than we needed, so now is the time to really get rid of these things.

43. Rework old methods of organization. If you are having to declutter a ton of stuff, the old methods clearly do not work anymore.

44. Putting things in storage does not equate to minimalism. Some people might shove different products in their cabinets in the hopes of

clearing counter space. If you use your blender or crockpot often, it is fine to keep it out on the counter and use that cabinet spot for something else that takes up unnecessary space.

45. Get rid of old Christmas lights. You might buy new decorations every year, so anything that can be easily replaced should be recycled if you do not really think you will use it anyway.

46. Invest in more than one trashcan. Some people might just have one in their kitchen, but you should keep small trash spots in your bedroom, the bathroom, and maybe even the living room. These should be used for things like receipts, notes, tissues, or other trash that would not smell. This stuff is better put in the trash can than on a pile on your desk or dresser.

47. Get rid of old games that you do not play. You might even have old puzzles and games sitting

around that are missing pieces. There is no reason to keep these.

48. Puzzles should be traded amongst friends as well. How often do you really do a puzzle more than once? Instead of buying more puzzles, just trade with your friends to get a new variety.

49. Unsubscribe from emails and newsletters. If you get junk mail, before recycling, see if there is a number you can call so that you can stop receiving mail from them. Many people overlook this and just toss the mail, only to get it again next month. The same goes for your online mail as well.

50. There is usually a link at the end of the email that you can quickly select to unsubscribe you from junk emails and promotions with just one click.

Chapter 5 – Implementing Minimalism

A t this point in the book, you should have a comprehensive idea of how to become a minimalist and some tips to help you easily get started. Everyone's minimalist journey is going to be different. It might mean starting tomorrow, you no longer allow yourself to impulsively make any purchases. It could also mean that tomorrow, you throw away everything except for 100 items.

This last chapter will go over more ideas of how to really incorporate minimalism, as well as some extra tips for a stress-free life and home. Once you make the decision to become a minimalist and then go through other steps to purge yourself of all your stuff, you will already feel better there. The journey does not stop there, however. You have to be consistent and keep up with different minimal habits in order to ensure that you do not fall back into healthy patterns that landed you in an unhappy spot in the first place.

Color Pallets

One thing that can help with minimalist design,

whether it is in fashion or in your home, is to choose a color pallet you like. Stick to colors that make you feel good, which might include neutral tones or soft, pastel colors. Maybe you like things that are vibrant because they bring about feelings of energy and alertness. We all have our preferences when it comes to different colors and sticking to things you like can really help you grow your minimalist style and identity.

If something does not fit in with your color pallet, there is a chance you might not want it in your life. Do not include things you do not enjoy just for the sake of variety. Stay strict with what you choose to bring into your home, and sometimes, you might even have to be a little hard on yourself.

Pick color pallets that are calming and neutral so that they can be interchanged with each other. Study some color design when painting your home and buying furniture. Just because red is your favorite color does not mean you should paint your walls red.

Instead, maybe you would be better off incorporating red accents throughout your home. Be smart when making color decisions so that you can ensure you're going to have results that make you feel good, and not ones that make you feel distracted.

Having specific "themes" can be limiting and a way to date things quickly. If you create a guide of the colors you like, you can better limit your stuff. Do not be too strict with labels. Sometimes, you might get sick of a certain style or theme if you try to stay too true to that idea. Sometimes less is more, and it is important to resist the urge to go overboard.

Cooking Minimally

Minimal eating habits are a great way for people to implement minimalism as well. Not only will it become easier to start eating a minimalist diet on your overall lifestyle, but you might find that you're much healthier than before. Not being a minimalist does not indicate that you're not healthy, however, there is a lot to be learned from a minimalist that is very conscious of the things they buy to cook and eat.

Create a pantry that gives you plenty of options. Stock up on pasta, grains, nuts, seeds, dried fruits, and other things that will last a long time. Even though minimalists know that less is more, they will usually purchase things in bulk. This allows for you to make sure you always keep variety in the kitchen. The more options you give yourself, the less likely it is you will find yourself going out and getting takeout.

Aside from building a big pantry, also be aware of other ways you can keep food in your life in a functional way with purpose and intent. Take fruit or veggies that are going bad and pickle them with vinegar or cook them in sugar to make jelly. Find a use and purpose in every food you purchase rather than just chucking it at the first sign of bruising.

Buy frozen veggies and fruit if you have to as well in order to keep healthy options around in your house. Eating healthy allows you to clear your brain and have a more focused mind. When you have all the supplies needed in your kitchen to make different meals, you have the ability to reduce the energy that goes into grocery shopping and meal planning.

For instance, someone that buys their groceries week to week might make a list of all the things that they need based around 4 or 5 recipes. They have to think about all of these specific ingredients, and then if they forget something at the store, that can ruin all their plans.

Instead of trying to plan meals week to week, fill your kitchen with everything that you might need so that you have more options than just what you think of on Mondays before you go to the grocery store. You can keep everything stocked so that you only have to buy minimal groceries when it comes time to head to the store. The better knowledge you have of cooking, the better off you will be in the long run of eating minimally.

You can also consider filling your home or garden with edible plants. Herbs are fairly simple to take care of and can be grown inside. You might also try growing different greens like lettuce or spinach in order to always have the option to eat a salad. Not only will these plants provide you with food, but they will also be great decorations around your home!

Minimal meals do not have to be boring. They are just consistent of whole foods and things that serve a purpose rather than just junk to fill your stomach. You will find so much more fulfillment from cooking your own meal than if you just keep microwaving TV dinners week after week.

Inspiring Family

It can be hard to be the only minimalist in a world full of people that are constantly wasting things. Seeing the way that other people live might make you want to go back to your old ways. In times that you're feeling down or going through something challenging, it can be hard to not look at people on social media or in the real world that have a lot of stuff and seem to be happier because of it.

When we're feeling sad, our brain is just trying to rationalize our emotions while looking for solutions. You might see these other people living with all their stuff and think, "I want that," but remind yourself this is not the way to achieve fulfillment. There is a reason you decided to become a minimalist in the first place so do not let yourself continue to be distracted with the desire for more.

You will realize that as you live your life, more people might become inspired. Others might see a difference in your overall level of happiness and wonder what you've been doing to make your life so much better. When you share your ideas on minimalism, others can catch on and see real-world examples of how these methods are effective. It can also be nice to help other people on their journey, as it will remind you again how important your own path has been.

Anyone that tries to criticize you about your lifestyle just needs to do some self-evaluation. There might be people that insult you on minimalist design choices or those that make you feel like what you're doing is dumb.

Any person that makes you feel bad about yourself is just trying to distract from their own flaws. We're all entitled to our own opinions, but do not let what other people think become your basis of reality. What you're doing is hard work, and that person that is criticizing you might just not be ready to start their own journey yet, and that is just fine.

 **Actionable Tip:** Throw a minimal party in which all of your friends or family members have to bring five items that they want to give away. Everyone at the party can take home whatever they want, but only three items at the most. Everything that is leftover can be donated!

Stay consistent with your lifestyle even if it seems like everyone is against you. Maybe your family is really involved in Black Friday shopping, and so on Thanksgiving Day, everyone talks about all the things they plan on buying.

It can be hard to not give in and join them but remember to stay true to your beliefs and values. You could still go shopping with them if you believe it would be a fun experience that might bring you closer but stay strong when you see all the sale signs. Nowadays, Black Friday sales are not even that great as stores know that people will be out shopping. They just use those words, "Black Friday," because they've become symbols that mean "discounted the most."

Minimal Advice

As a minimalist, you will of course want to encourage other people to follow your same lifestyle. As a person living a happy life, it can be hard not to tell others that they should live like you, so they can be happy too! When you've truly started to experience a happy and joy-filled life, you want to share it with the world!

Minimalists know the value in family and they hold their loved ones very close. Why would we not want these people we love so much to be as happy as us? As a minimalist, however, you need to apply that same level of reduction to the advice you try to give others.

No one likes being told what to do, so it is best if you let people become minimal at their own pace. If all you do is talk about how great your life is now, people will tune you out. It can be hard for unhappy people to really listen to the words of those around them that appear to be happier.

No one likes a gloater. Instead, when discussing your current life, wait for them to ask questions in order to see what areas of curiosity they have. Make sure you ask questions as well, not necessarily to gain any information, but to give the other person a chance to talk and discuss their thoughts and feelings on minimalism.

Remember that everyone goes at their own pace and not all people will be able to ever achieve minimalism. You have to remember that this is completely fine, and just because you've found peace through minimalism does not mean that someone else will. It seems like the truest and simplest way to achieve peace and happiness, but not everyone has the strength to look at their past traumas and childhood to confront the deeper issues needed to overcome in order to get a minimalist mindset.

If someone is ready to become minimal, then help them with the information they need to find success with the lifestyle. Do not try to dictate someone else's life, and make sure that you're not making them do anything that makes them feel uncomfortable. Be there to help them with whatever they need but do your best not to "lead" them, as a minimalist journey is about finding your own peace and answers.

Do not Be too Controlling

Do not tell others how to live their life. Do not be mean to someone that still buys a lot of plastic junk. They might really like having novelty items around. Just because you do not find happiness from a certain item does not mean that others can't either. They might find pure joy in the objects that they buy, and that is not for you to decide or change.

Do not shame someone that is not living minimally. There are some people that do not have the financial means to buy quality items, so they might just have to shop at discount stores that make cheap things that break easily. Others might still have to buy fast food because of their budget and busy lifestyle.

While you might not agree with their practices, know that they are just in a different stage of their life. They are not the people you should be angry with. Instead, it is the fault of manufacturers and CEOs of mega-corporations that continually make others feel as though they need to make certain purchases as a form of compensation.

If you feel the need to control others, remember to look inward. If someone else's lifestyle is making you stressed out or anxious, ask why. Sometimes, it is because we love people and want what is best for them, but they have to discover what is best for them on their own. You do not get to make that definition. Before becoming minimalist, you probably had trouble getting started or even considering getting rid of your stuff in the first place. Remember what it was like before you started and use that knowledge to be empathetic to others that are just trying to get through their day to day life.

Personal Environments

The environments that surround us can pose some serious challenges when it comes to maintaining minimalism. Especially if we live in an area full of industrialized businesses, or worse, work in a place that constantly offers discounts. Do not let these challenges become your areas of weakness.

Use these chances of temptation to look inward and study yourself, figuring out why you might feel the need to give into your surroundings. You can also use the chance of temptation to study what makes other people choose to not be a minimalist. Maybe you work in a department store and have to stare at cheap clothes all day that you could buy for even less after employee discounts. Ask yourself, do the customers coming in always seem happier after they leave? Sometimes, people are just generally happy, but is it because of their purchase?

Also, use your downtime to look at the advertisements around you. Study the way sales signs are written and what their placement might be in the store. Identify the different techniques used to make you feel like you have to buy the item on the sale rack.

Your space is what should inspire you, so if you feel like you are in a space that is too cluttered, it is okay to remove yourself. After becoming minimalist, you just might have to find a new job that does not require you to be surrounded by so much temptation. You might have groups of friends that live very indulgent lifestyles, and it is okay to cut them out or reduce your time together if it means that you will become healthier and find more personal growth.

You do not have to be mean to anyone, or never talk to them again. However, if you're friends with a bunch of people that all sell things from businesses like Mary Kay or other small businesses that allow representatives to work for them, you might need to avoid going to their selling parties.

Make sure to still compromise with roommates or spouses that do not have the same ideas. There are ways to subtly include minimalism. You can't dictate someone else's space, so if they have a bunch of stuff, it is not up to you to give their things away. We'll talk more about living with a non-minimalist in the next chapter.

It is important to understand how one can better live in their personal environment as a minimalist. Always remember to do what is best for you and stop a temptation before it becomes a bad habit that you regret.

Living with a Non-Minimalist

Living with someone that is not a minimalist might be challenging, especially if they are your partner. Maybe they have an overflowing closet and you just have five items. Having to look at someone else's stuff can also be stressful, especially if you're just starting out becoming a minimalist. When you decide to go on this journey, you should do your best to include your spouse, partner, roommate, or closest friend, if they are not minimalists already.

Pretty much anyone can benefit from minimalism, so you should do your best to make sure that you're encouraging those around you to join in on the journey. Spouses might even find their relationships improving if they become minimalists together.

Remember that you still can't dictate how someone else lives their life. Instead of being too controlling, remember to practice patience and mindfulness. They are not your responsibility at the end of the day, so if they do not want to become a minimalist, you can't make them.

Take turns cooking minimal meals and encourage them to downsize their stuff. Encourage them to help you out when it comes time to declutter. Ask permission for decluttering their things to see if they would let you help them declutter. If someone does not want to, however, you have to learn to accept that.

Remember that you do not have control over other people's things. Even if it seems as though they have a shirt they've never worn, it is not your decision to throw it away. If someone wants to keep extra junk they do not need, you can't tell them that they have to throw it away.

Minimalism in a High-Paced World

Our world is certainly not minimal. It can sometimes be lonely to look at all the ways other people consume at such high levels. All around us there are non-minimalists that keep buying things they do not need just to find some form of happiness. It might be hard to see but remember that not everyone that is purchasing things is unhappy. Some people are completely content with their life and have never even considered the idea of minimalism.

If you feel as though you can't keep up, find an

online community that shares your opinions. Remember that you're not alone in this journey even if it feels as though everyone around you is just throwing away their money in exchange for plastic junk.

Remember to continually analyze the messages that different companies are trying to sell. The manipulation tactics of marketers and advertisers is only going to get stronger as our lives go on in this world of innovation. Be ready to combat any emotions elicited by an advertisement. At the end of the day, it just exists to get you to buy something.

Maintaining Minimalism

Once minimalism is achieved, it can be simple for some people to maintain this behavior. The minimalist mindset might be like a lightbulb that goes on and never shuts off. Once you realize that the things that surround you are not going to be the answer to happiness, you might never be able to go back to the way things used to be.

Some people might feel as though they do not have control over their life, so minimalism will help. It could be challenging at first, but practice makes perfect no matter what the context.

Remember it all starts with your mindset. At the end of the day, it is what is in your head that matters the most, in terms of how you're going to properly achieve your goals.

 **Actionable Tip:** Keep a diary of your moods and emotions. Track what you did in a day and what your mood throughout the day is. You will find you are happier in times that were spent with experiencing things rather than obsessing over material objects. When it can feel hard to maintain minimalism, check back in with this diary to remind yourself that it is all worth it in the end!

Conclusion

T hroughout this book, the main things that you should have learned were:

1. What minimalism is

2. Why minimalism is important

3. How minimalism can change your life

4. How to get started with a minimalist path

The rest is going to be up to you. This can be the scariest part for some people. You can read the book over and over again, but it is not going to mean anything if you do not actually try to apply these ideas and standards to your life.

You need to stay strict, make plans, and set goals

for everything that you wish to achieve through minimalism. The learning does not have to stop here either. Check out other books on minimalism and look into notable blogs that cover the topic. The more you know, the better you will understand minimalism, which will make it much easier for you to actually apply certain information to your life.

The most important first step to getting to a place where you're happier has to be changing the way you perceive the world. You have to gain a new perspective on what is important and what is not. Look for purpose and intent within everything that you do. The thoughts that cross through your mind and the feelings that you have all derive from somewhere important. It is up to you what you're going to do with those thoughts now.

Thoughts are just that; things that you think. You

can't always stop them from happening, and you should never feel guilty about the first thing that you think. What is most important now, however, in your journey, is choosing what you're going to do with those thoughts. You can either let them control your life, or you can ignore them, putting focus and attention on the things that really matter most.

Staying on the Minimalist Path

If you have moments of weakness when you just want to buy a bunch of stuff, that is completely fine. Do not beat yourself up because you fell for a marketing scheme. They are designed to trick and manipulate us, so it is not always your fault that you got manipulated. Be realistic and honest with yourself, however. Do not choose to ignore clear signs that something should not be purchased just because it is easier to give into the sale or the price tag. If you have a moment of weakness, do not ruminate for too long. You could let one mistake ruin your day if you think about it over and over and over again. Instead of wishing that you hadn't done something in the first place, put that energy into seeing how you could turn that moment into a learning opportunity.

Evaluate what first triggered the old feelings of wanting to buy something. Maybe an upcoming wedding made you go all out on the right outfit even though you do not even personally know the bride or groom.

Once you have identified what caused you to make an impulsive or non-minimalist decision, figure out what you can do in the future to make sure that this does not happen again. Ask yourself how you could have avoided the situation, and what you might have needed in order to stop the purchase from happening in the first place.

Do not ever let yourself stop questioning intent or purpose. It might seem overwhelming to do so much searing, but it's what is needed to be done in order to achieve a happier and more fulfilling life.

There is no such thing as "relapsing," in terms of owning stuff. As long as you keep it consistent and cut bad behavior short, you will likely be able to stay on the minimalist path. If you do "relapse" more than once a week, however, you're likely just letting yourself partake in old bad habits that didn't work in the first place! Correct your behavior and know that you're allowed to make mistakes.

Be easy on yourself in difficult scenarios as well. If you went through a huge breakup, maybe going on a shopping spree could help out. It is okay to seek momentary relief when you're going through an especially challenging moment. At the end of the day, however, remember that this is not what is going to heal the wound. It might just act as the pain reliever needed while the wound heals.

Remember to reach out to others and continue to do research on minimalist methods in order to learn new ways to keep your life simple. If you are feeling alone in your minimalist journey, remember that someone else out there is likely feeling the same way. You do not have to do it alone, even if no one else in your family has the desire to become a minimalist. There are others that are trying to better themselves, and maybe even the world, with minimalism, so you do not have to feel like you have to carry all the weight.

Habits of Success to Follow

The biggest step to take as a minimalist is to stop meaningless purchases. Right now, make a promise to yourself that you are not going to buy anything you do not need. Do not say, "Oh, I'll start my new shopping habits next week." You know what is going to happen? Next week is going to come around and there'll be a sale you just can't resist, so then you will say again, "Oh, I'll start my new shopping habits next week." Then it is the third week and there is another reason why you can't start your new journey. Do not put this process off. If living a more clear-minded, simple life sounds interesting to you at all, then remember you're going to have to stop your bad habits right in this moment. You can't expect to have a positive change from a consistent lifestyle that has not been working for you already.

Next, go through your stuff and choose what should be kept versus tossed. This does not have to be done rapidly, and you should make sure you're going at your own pace and at a speed you're comfortable with in order to make sure that you do not end up making yourself miserable. If you start off really hard and make yourself really unhappy from the beginning, you're going to come to hate minimalism!

Do you know why people always struggle to diet or exercise? They think they can just start right away with the habits of someone that is been dieting and exercising for years. If going to McDonald's and 7-11 is a regular thing, you can't just stop going one week and force yourself to eat kale salads even though you hate kale. The important thing to remember is that it might be a gradual process.

Cold turkey works for some people, but do not feel bad if you're not "some people." If you torture yourself with minimalism, you will grow to hate it just like how someone that tries to extreme diet will grow to hate kale.

To keep up with this, throw things away right away if you do end up buying them. Keep receipts around so that you can return things if you have a slip-up. Sit on a purchase for a couple of days if you must, questioning if you're actually happier or more fulfilled now that you made that purchase in the first place.

Testing Minimalism

Start by testing out different areas of minimalism in your life before forcing yourself to stick to one method. Instead of throwing all of your clothes away, pick out the ones that you want to keep the most. Try living with just those clothes for a week, or maybe a month, just to see if you're okay with living with less clothing.

There are some people that are legitimately passionate about fashion, so they might not always find happiness from purging themselves of clothes. If after that week or month you didn't even think about wearing something else, you can rest assured knowing that you're not going to miss those clothes once they've been donated.

The same kind of testing can be done if you want to give away your books or movies. Box them up and set the boxes aside. If after a month the boxes have remained unopen, you know that you can just give them away and you will not miss them as much as you might have feared.

Staying Fluid with Minimalism

Minimalism is strict for some people, but you can also be very relaxed and casual with how much you allow this idea into your life. Staying very strict and rigid with your rules might be what you need in order to succeed. You might also still find happiness by just playing around with a few different types of minimalism.

Do not be too hard on yourself and do what works best for you. At the end of the day, the goal is to just be happy, and only you have the power to define what it is going to take for you to achieve your goals.

About the Author

Mary Connor is a professional organizer, a wife and mom to three children, a cleaning expert, and a former finance manager. She is passionate about helping people lead better lives and shares easy and inexpensive organizing tips and tricks on how to clean up life's little and big messes. In addition, she teaches women how to pay off debts, improve their money management skills and increase their wealth.

In the past, Mary found her passion in writing and focuses on topics that can make a real difference in helping others accomplish their goals and dreams. She has made it a habit to continue learning new things so that she can share these insights with the world in a concise and helpful way. This interest has led her to the life of learning several factors affecting human interactions. Moreover, she continually works on expanding her knowledge by attending seminars and networking with other professionals.

Mary loves the outdoors and likes to walk or run every day. She is dedicated to the practice of mindfulness and feels that a minimalist lifestyle is important to both success and happiness. When not writing or walking, Mary enjoys spending time horseback riding with her daughters or relaxing at the lake with her husband.

www.ingramcontent.com/pod-product-compliance
Lightning Source LLC
Chambersburg PA
CBHW020238130626
46549CB00005B/1949